# MURDER & MAYHEM
## — IN —
## SOUTHEAST
# KANSAS

# MURDER & MAYHEM
## — IN —
## SOUTHEAST
# KANSAS

## LARRY E. WOOD

THE
History
PRESS

Published by The History Press
Charleston, SC
www.historypress.com

*Front cover, top*: from the *St. Louis Republic*; *bottom*: Kansas State Historical Society.
*Back cover*: Kansas State Historical Society; *inset*: from the *St. Paul Globe*.

First published 2019

Manufactured in the United States

ISBN 9781467141406

Library of Congress Control Number: 2018963660

# CONTENTS

# CONTENTS

# ACKNOWLEDGEMENTS

A lthough much of my research for this book was done online, I still did quite a bit of it the old-fashioned way, and I want to thank Jason Sullivan and Patty Crane, reference librarians at the Joplin Public Library, for fulfilling my interlibrary loan requests.

I'd like to thank Kristine Schmucker, curator of the Harvey County Historical Museum and Archives, for her insight into the Newton gunfight and for helping me with my research on that topic. I also thank her and the museum for providing a pertinent photograph.

I appreciate the timely manner in which Nancy Sherbert, photo archivist at the Kansas State Historical Society, responded to my several requests for photos from that organization.

I wish to thank Lindsey Givens, commissioning editor with Arcadia Publishing/The History Press, for her prompt and helpful answers to my inquiries as I prepared the manuscript and gathered the images for this book. I also appreciate copyeditor Rick Delaney's thorough proofreading and editing of the manuscript. His attention to detail has resulted in a more polished and professional finished product.

# 1

# DEADLY DAY IN LADORE

## A QUINTUPLE LYNCHING

O n Tuesday, May 10, 1870, seven young men rode into Ladore, Kansas, looking to raise hell. The men were drawn by Ladore's rough-and-tumble reputation as a place where whiskey flowed freely and rowdy behavior generally went unchecked. But there were some things even the people of Ladore would not abide. When the seven young hellions got liquored up and crossed the line, only one made it out of town alive.[1]

Located in southern Neosho County about six miles north of present-day Parsons, Ladore was, in the spring of 1870, a booming little town slated to become a junction point of the Missouri, Kansas and Texas Railroad (aka the Katy). The place pulsed with boisterous activity in anticipation of the road's completion, and all manner of debauchery and incivility found a home. "Dramshops have multiplied," complained a local resident at the time, "and drunken rowdies have become so bold that decent people are almost afraid to show their faces on the streets."[2]

More than thirty years later, L.A. Bowes, foreman of the construction crew that was building the railroad, remembered the town in similar but more colorful terms. "All the Wild Bills, Texas Jacks, Buckskin Joes and Alkali Ikes seemed to have congregated there," he recalled. "It was the toughest place...I ever struck. Whisky was sold in nearly every house in the town. Vice and immorality flourished like a green bay tree."[3]

The seven young men, identified initially only as "Texans or straggling outlaws from the Indian Territory," hit town about noon, according to Bowes, and "commenced to fill up on tangleleg." Heavily armed, the men took entire possession of the town. By evening, they started knocking people down and robbing them, firing off their pistols indiscriminately, and "raising the devil" generally.[4]

About 9:00 p.m., the seven men went to the boardinghouse of James N. Roach, a quarter-mile south of town near the railroad right-of-way and asked for rooms. Seeing their state of intoxication, Roach told them he didn't have any rooms for them, but they retorted that they would stay anyway. The "hardened wretches" hit Roach with their pistols, knocking him down and leaving him for dead, as they presumed.[5]

The "hell-prompted villains" then turned their attention to the female quarters on the bottom floor of the two-story building, where Roach's nineteen-year-old daughter, Sophia, and two hired girls, fourteen-year-old Jane Talbott and her thirteen-year-old sister, Alice Talbott, roomed. A number of railroad workers were staying on the second floor, and two of the hellions guarded the outside stairs that led to the workmen's quarters to prevent them from interfering while the other five men stalked toward the girls' room. Sophia made her escape by slipping into an adjoining room and hiding, but the drunken scoundrels dragged the Talbott sisters from their room and herded them outside, where they took turns raping them.[6]

Still stunned but conscious, Roach could hear the screams of the young girls, but he dared not stir for fear that the men would kill him. During the night, an argument erupted among the desperadoes over one of the girls, and the leader of the gang shot and killed one of his own men.[7]

Finally, the crying and screaming of the younger girl became so heartrending that even one of the gang members took pity on her and returned her to the boardinghouse. Meanwhile, the men "brutally outraged and ravished the other."[8]

Shortly after midnight, the villains broke up. One of the gang members took the Talbott girl to the nearby Labette Creek woods, where he wrapped her and himself in a blanket and soon fell asleep. Three others deemed it prudent to head out of town, and they started northeast on the Osage Mission road. The remaining two went looking for more liquor. Meanwhile, Roach finally ventured to give an alarm.[9]

The two thirsty desperadoes called at The Inn, a boardinghouse in Ladore run by James Abell. They found Susan Abell and her daughters, fifteen-year-old Sarah Matilda and twelve-year-old Elizabeth, there alone, because Jim Abell had already answered the alarm and was out looking for the rapists with a posse of Ladore's other male citizens. The Inn was closed, but the ruffians started breaking in. Susan picked up an ax and herded her daughters up a ladder into an unfinished attic. When the desperadoes gained entrance into the house and tried to follow the females into the attic, Susan fended them off with the ax, and they finally gave up and turned their attention to the liquor they'd come for.[10]

About daylight, the posse, now swollen to almost three hundred men, found the man who'd taken Jane Talbott to the woods, still curled up in his blanket with the girl. They first tried to hang him with a grapevine, but it broke. They then procured a rope and strung him up to a limb of a hackberry tree on the bank of Labette Creek.[11]

Near the same time, the two desperadoes who'd gone to Abell's boardinghouse were found there in a drunken stupor. They were taken to the local barbershop, a log building, and guarded there momentarily, then brought down to the Roach place, where the Talbott girls identified them as two of the party who had attacked them. They were promptly strung up side by side on the same limb as their comrade.[12]

Sometime after daylight, the other three men were overtaken on the Osage Mission road and brought back to Ladore. They, too, were marched before the Talbott girls, who identified two of them as participants in the previous night's crime. Alice Talbott said the third man was the one who'd taken her back to the boardinghouse, and both girls agreed that he did not participate in the hellish deeds of the other six men. Identified as Peter Kelly, he was placed under guard pending further investigation, while his two partners soon adorned the hackberry tree alongside the other three men. It was not yet 11:00 a.m. on May 11, 1870.[13]

Before they were launched into eternity, the lynching victims gave their names as William Ryan of Illinois, Patrick Starr of New York, Patsey Riley of Massachusetts, Richard Pilbin of Missouri, and Alexander Mathews of Canada. The man who'd been shot by the gang leader was identified as Robert Wright.[14]

The men's bodies were left hanging for several hours, and most of the residents of Ladore took the opportunity to amble down to Labette Creek and gawk at the gruesome ornaments dangling from the hackberry tree. About 3:00 p.m., county coroner Stephen Carr arrived, and the bodies were cut down and laid out beneath the tree. Very little effort was made, however, to identify the vigilantes who'd done the lynching, perhaps because virtually all the adult men of Ladore had participated, either directly or indirectly, in the extralegal action. "No official of the law ever asked any questions about the hanging or in any way interfered with those engaged in it," Bowes recalled years later. Instead, the jury came to the hasty and rather

From *The Katy Railroad and the Last Frontier. Used by permission, University of Oklahoma Press.*

meaningless conclusion that the five men who'd been hanged had come to their deaths by strangulation at the hands of parties unknown.[15]

The man who'd been shot, added the jury, came to his death by a pistol shot from an unknown person, inflicted while the deceased was attempting to commit a rape. After the inquest, all six of the dead outlaws were dumped into a large hole that had been dug near the hackberry tree and buried there in a common grave.[16]

Sheriff Michael Barnes showed up at or near the same time as the coroner, while the vigilantes were still debating what to do about Peter Kelly. Barnes took charge of him and escorted him to Osage Mission. He was temporarily lodged in the city jail there and later transferred to the Allen County Jail at Iola. He and several other prisoners escaped from the Iola jail in July, but Kelly was soon recaptured. Charges against him for his part in the Ladore tragedy were eventually dropped.[17]

Doctors who treated the Talbott girls reported them in critical condition. It was thought that the younger of the two, who was torn and terribly cut with a knife, could not survive, but she recovered and lived at least into adulthood. The older girl died in July 1871, when she was barely sixteen years old, although it's not known whether her ordeal at the hands of the Ladore villains just over a year earlier contributed to her premature demise.[18]

Editorial observers were swift to uphold the action of the Ladore vigilantes. "The citizens of Ladore deserve the thanks of every decent person," said the *Chetopa Advance*, "for hanging these vile scoundrels, who, by their acts have thrown the atrocities of the savage Indian into the shade." While generally

Ladore Cemetery is about the only sign left that the community ever existed. *Photo by the author.*

in agreement with the *Advance*'s sentiment, the *Osage Mission Journal* was more circumspect: "We exceedingly regret that any person should deem it necessary to take the lives of human beings 'without due process of law.' Heretofore we have borne the reputation of being a law-abiding people. If the people of Ladore have forfeited it, they certainly had grave reasons for their proceedings. If justification is possible, *they are justified.* 'The way of the transgressor is hard.'"[19]

After the five desperadoes were lynched, according to Bowes, "Ladore became a good, moral town. Everyone seemed to be on his good behavior. The Wild Bills, Texas Jacks, Buckskin Joes and Alkali Ikes left for more congenial climes and the town settled into a quiet, peaceful village."[20]

Alas, Ladore's prosperity was short lived. The first passenger train, running on the Neosho Division of the Katy, reached Ladore on May 21, ten days after the lynchings, but the main line of the railroad ultimately bypassed Ladore. Instead, Parsons, six miles to the south, was chosen as the junction point, and it prospered in Ladore's place. A number of Ladore residents even picked up and moved to Parsons. Ladore gradually declined until 1901, when it lost its post office, after which it soon vanished into a ghost town. Today, about the only sign that Ladore ever existed is the Ladore Cemetery, located on an out-of-the-way, dead-end road in southern Neosho County.[21]

# 2

# THE HIDE PARK GUNFIGHT

## ONE OF THE "BLOODIEST AFFRAYS" EVER

I n the wee hours of Sunday morning, August 20, 1871, one of the deadliest shootouts in the history of the Wild West broke out at Perry Tuttle's dance hall in the Hide Park section of Newton, Kansas. When the gunfire ceased, one person was dead, at least two more had fatal wounds, and as many as seven others were nursing injuries that ranged from critical to slight.[22]

The exact details of what happened are fuzzy, because initial reports tended to be vague or contradictory. And it doesn't help that the reporter who wrote the most thorough firsthand account of the episode later turned out to be a shyster given not only to embellishing the truth but also to inventing stories entirely.

Still, it's safe to say, as the *Emporia Weekly News* observed in the aftermath of the incident, that the Newton gunfight was "one of the bloodiest affrays that ever occurred" in the state of Kansas.[23]

Newton sprang up almost overnight along the Chisholm Trail about twenty-five miles north of Wichita in the late spring of 1871 in anticipation of the Atchison, Topeka and Santa Fe Railroad intersecting the trail at that point later in the year. When the railroad reached the place in mid-July, Newton immediately became a booming cattle town, displacing Abilene as the primary shipping point for herds driven up the Chisholm Trail. By late July, Newton boasted a population of five hundred people, and carload after carload of Texas cattle shipped out of the Newton stockyards every day headed for eastern markets.[24]

By mid-August, the population had ballooned to fifteen hundred, according to one estimate, and homes and businesses, many of them catering to the Texas cowboys, were going up apace. Among the businesses were eight gambling institutions and twenty-seven places where liquor was sold. There was not a school or church in the town "nor…even a religious organization."[25]

One corner of the town site away from the main district and south of the railroad tracks was set aside "for abandoned women." The place consisted of two dance halls and several surrounding houses that were used "for purposes which the reader can divine without unnecessary explanation." This red-light district was dubbed Hide Park, supposedly because of the amount of "hide" the women at the dancing establishments showed. Half a dozen women inhabited each dance hall, and customers were expected to buy drinks for themselves and their partners at the conclusion of each dance. "At all hours of the night, and on Sundays, may be heard the music of the orchestras and the hippity-hoppity of the dancers," said one observer. "The girls get drunk, shout, swear and make exhibitions too indecent for description."[26]

Newton's inhabitants included "some of the most uncouth and reckless men in the world," and since the town had no city government, it had to

Main Street of Newton, Kansas, circa 1871. *Kansas State Historical Society.*

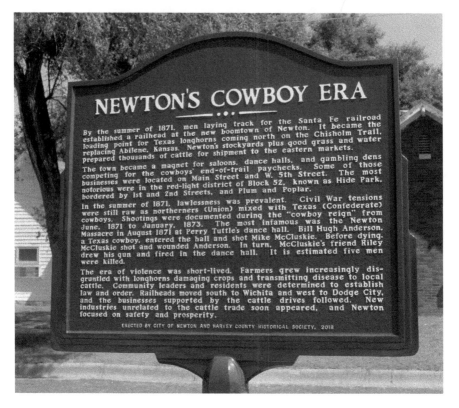

Historical marker commemorating Newton's rowdy cow town days. *Courtesy Harvey County Historical Society.*

depend on a county deputy and two township constables to maintain law and order. Special policemen were also appointed on occasion and paid from funds taken out of gambling proceeds.[27]

A bond to decide whether a railroad would be extended to Wichita was scheduled for a vote on Friday, August 11, and Texan Bill Bailey and railroad man William McCluskie were appointed to serve as Newton special policemen during the election. They were supposed to keep the peace, but they ended up causing more trouble than they prevented. Bailey had reportedly killed a couple of men in Texas, and McCluskie, who'd recently been released from an arrest on a garroting charge, was also a hard case. According to one report, Bailey became domineering toward the "shorthorns," or non-Texans, in Newton and started abusing McCluskie in particular. Other accounts, however, say that the two men had been feuding for some time over a woman and over McCluskie's recent arrest. In any case, the two men argued on Election Day, and late that night the quarrel exploded into a drunken fistfight at the Red Front Saloon. Carrying the dispute outside, the two faced each other on the street, and McCluskie drew his revolver and shot Bailey. He died the next day, and McCluskie fled town to avoid arrest, even though many townspeople thought Bailey got what he deserved. When the fugitive learned that no effort was being made to apprehend him, he returned a few days later.[28]

The Texans swarming the cow town of Newton didn't share the opinion of the permanent residents that Bailey deserved the fate he received, and they vowed revenge on McCluskie. A Texan named Hugh Anderson was especially keen on making McCluskie pay for killing Bailey. In the wee hours of Sunday morning, August 20, barely a week since his shootout with Bailey, McCluskie was partaking of "the licentious and wicked festivities" at Perry Tuttle's dance hall across the tracks when the owner announced it was closing time. McCluskie and a number of other customers continued to loiter, and two or three of Anderson's sidekicks shuffled in. Tuttle was still trying to clear the place out when Anderson himself came in. Confronting McCluskie, Anderson called him a "cowardly son of a bitch." McCluskie sprang up, and the two men drew their pistols and started shooting at each other. The firing almost immediately became general as the allies of each man joined in the fray.[29]

At least one of Anderson's shots found its mark, but the seriously wounded McCluskie continued discharging his pistol. One of his shots or that of one of his cohorts hit Texan James Martin, who was trying to intervene to keep the peace. Martin fell dead, shot through the jugular vein. When McCluskie finally slumped to the floor, Anderson stalked over and shot him again.[30]

According to R.W.P. Muse's "History of Harvey County," written ten years after the gunfight, an eighteen-year-old lad named Riley, who was dying of consumption and whom McCluskie had befriended, was standing at the door during the initial barrage. When the gunfire died down, he coolly locked the door and started shooting his friend's assailants, killing Martin and Billy Garrett outright and wounding three other cowboys. Riley no doubt did participate in the shootout, but it seems more likely that the gunfire became general almost immediately, as some contemporaneous reports indicated, than that young Riley dramatically locked the door and singlehandedly felled half a dozen adversaries after the firing had hit a lull. It's a good story, but it seems like romantic exaggeration.[31]

When the smoke in Tuttle's dance hall cleared, Martin was dead, McCluskie lay dying, and at least six other men had wounds of varying severity. McCluskie was carried to an upstairs room as both Tuttle's place and its neighboring rival, the Alamo, were turned into makeshift hospitals. Two doctors were summoned to treat the wounded, and the dance girls assumed roles as nurses.[32]

McCluskie, who revealed on his deathbed that his real name was Arthur Delaney, lingered several hours before dying about 8:00 a.m. Sunday morning, August 21. Later that morning, Coroner C.S. Bowman held an inquest over the bodies of Martin and McCluskie (aka Delaney). The jury found that Martin had come to his death at the hands of an unknown person. McCluskie, on the other hand, had died from a shot fired by Hugh Anderson, feloniously and with intent to kill.[33]

A correspondent to the *New York World*, styling himself "Allegro," was on the scene in Newton and filed a thorough account of the Hide Park gunfight with the *Topeka Daily Commonwealth*. Allegro listed the men who were wounded but still alive as railroad brakeman Patrick Lee; another railroad man named Hickey; Texans Hugh Anderson, Billy Garrett, Henry Kearnes, and Jim Wilkerson; and at least one other unidentified cowpoke. Another report said Anderson's brother was also injured in the melee. Allegro listed Garrett's wounds as fatal and Lee's as critical, and they did later die according to at least two sources, although a conflicting report a couple of days after the shootout said Lee was on his way to recovery. Allegro also listed Kearnes as fatally wounded, but again a conflicting report said otherwise—that his wounds were slight. Adding credence to the contrary accounts, Muse recollected ten years after the deadly fracas that Garrett was the only man killed in the Hide Park gunfight besides Martin and McCluskie.[34]

A warrant for the arrest of Hugh Anderson was issued after the coroner's inquest, but before he could be taken into custody, he was whisked away to Kansas City with the aid of some of the citizens of Newton, who were glad to be rid of him. Anderson, whose wounds were not considered life-threatening, was nursed back to health in Kansas City, and he later returned to Texas and became a successful cattleman.[35]

Newton's boom as a cow town lasted only one season. By the spring of 1872, the railroad had reached Wichita, and it displaced Newton as the primary shipping point for cattle along the Chisholm Trail, just as Newton had displaced Abilene.

In the summer of 1873, Allegro, whose real name was E.J. Harrington, filed a story with the *New York World* claiming that a man named Arthur McCluskie had avenged his brother's death by killing Hugh Anderson in a duel at Medicine Lodge, Indian Territory. The fact that Medicine Lodge was in Kansas, not Indian Territory, might have aroused suspicion, because the supposed duel was quickly exposed as a complete fabrication. In a column branding Harrington as a shyster and a fraud shortly after the *New York World* story appeared, the *Topeka Daily Commonwealth* recalled him as "that cheerful Bohemian and dead-beat that wrote the lively 'Allegro' letters for the *Commonwealth* from Newton."[36]

So, the exact details of what happened at the Hide Park gunfight may never be known, but we know enough to say that it has rightly taken its place as one of the deadliest shootouts in the legend and lore of the Old West.

# THE STORY OF THE BLOODY BENDERS

## ONE OF THE GREAT UNSOLVED MYSTERIES OF THE OLD WEST

D r. William York left his home in Independence, Kansas, about the first of March 1873 to visit his parents in Fort Scott. He spent a few days in Fort Scott and left there on the morning of March 10 to return to Independence. He reached the Osage Mission safely but never made it home.[37]

York wasn't the first traveler in recent months to have disappeared mysteriously between Independence and the Osage Mission. On November 6 or 7, 1872, H.F. McKenzie started for Independence from a residence about twelve miles north of Cherryvale and went missing. On November 26, George Longcor and his baby girl started from their home west of Independence in a wagon to visit relatives in Iowa, intending to camp the first night on Drum Creek a few miles north of Cherryvale. No sign of the man and his daughter was found after that day until Longcor's bloodstained wagon turned up three months later a few miles away from his planned campsite. On November 30, Benjamin Brown left Osage Mission for his home in Howard County (now Elk and Chautauqua Counties) but never arrived. Two or three other people had disappeared under similar circumstances in the same general area.[38]

But it wasn't until Dr. York disappeared and his well-known brother, Kansas state senator Alexander M. York, became involved in searching for him that citizens and authorities alike became generally aroused by the mysterious disappearances. After a couple of weeks with no word from Dr. York, Senator York and another brother, Ed York, accompanied by a few

*Left*: Sketch of John Bender. *Right*: Sketch of Kate Bender. *Author's collection.*

other men, left Independence on March 24 to look for their missing brother. After first visiting Fort Scott to ascertain Dr. York's movements in that area, they started back toward Independence, following the same trail their brother had taken. Making inquiries along the way, they learned that the doctor had safely reached the Osage Mission and some few miles beyond, but after that, they lost all track of him.[39]

One of the places where the search party stopped was the Bender residence, located north of Cherryvale on the trail from Osage Mission to Independence between Drum Creek and Big Hill, the two most prominent landmarks along the barren stretch of road. The Benders' place served as a crude sort of roadside grocery where travelers could stop to rest and get a drink or a bite to eat. The family consisted of fifty-six-year-old John; his fifty-two-year-old wife, Mary; their twenty-six-year-old son, John; and their sixteen-year-old daughter, Kate. Originally from Germany, the family had lived a while in France, where Kate was born, before coming to the United States. They had moved to Kansas from Illinois just fifteen months earlier.[40]

Mature for her age, Kate claimed to be a spiritual medium and a doctor who could heal all manner of diseases, including blindness and deafness, and she advertised her services in local newspapers and on cards she distributed. When Senator York and his party stopped at the Bender residence on Wednesday, April 2, to inquire after the missing doctor, Kate told the senator that, if he would return on Friday, she would conduct a séance during which she would reveal the whereabouts of his brother. Young John Bender also offered to help, and he took the search party about three miles away from the house to a place where he said he'd been shot at the previous Christmas.[41]

Senator York and his companions dismissed Kate's claims of psychic power and went on their way without giving her and her curious family a second thought. The men returned to Independence without any solid leads into the mysterious disappearances, but they were convinced that Dr. York and the other missing persons had been cruelly murdered. Senator York offered a $100 reward for information leading to the discovery of his brother, either dead or alive, and Governor Thomas A. Osborn offered a $500 reward for the apprehension and conviction of the party or parties who'd killed Dr. York and the other missing persons.[42]

A month later, on Friday, May 2, Silas Toles, a neighbor of the Benders, was passing their place when he noticed that the premises had a desolate look, with cattle and hogs wandering around aimlessly as if they needed attention. Upon closer inspection, Toles found the home deserted, the family's wagon and team gone, and a dead calf in a nearby pen, apparently starved to death.[43]

Informed of Toles's findings on Monday, May 5, Ed York, accompanied by a township trustee and two detectives, trekked out to the Bender place that day and searched the house, which consisted of a single large room divided into two by a cloth partition. A stench emanated from beneath the floor, and the men located a trapdoor in the back room. When they took up the trap door, they found bloodstains but nothing more incriminating. The next day, they searched the grounds of an orchard southeast of the house, where the soil had been freshly plowed. York noticed a depression in the ground, and when a metal rod was thrust into the soil, it went in easily to a depth beyond the level disturbed by the plow. The men began digging and soon uncovered the body of Dr. York. His head had been bashed in on both sides and his throat slit from ear to ear.[44]

Two hammers were found in the house, and the business end of the instruments matched the death wounds on Dr. York's head. The next day, May 7, seven more bodies were uncovered, including those of H.F. McKenzie, Benjamin Brown, George Longcor, and his little girl. One or two other bodies were later discovered, and many people speculated that there might be more. All the victims had suffered wounds similar to York's except the child, who'd apparently been suffocated. The investigators' theory of the crimes was that the Benders induced their victims to sit in the front room with their backs to the partition so that their forms were visible in outline from the rear. Someone in the back room would strike the victims with one or more blows from a hammer, rendering them unconscious or

Bender house during the search for bodies, sketched from the adjacent photo or a similar one. *From* Harper's Weekly.

Photo of Bender house during the search for bodies. *Author's collection.*

stunning them until a knife could finish the deadly work. The bodies were then dropped through the trapdoor and were later taken from beneath the house via an outside access and buried. Robbery was the only motive that could be offered for the heinous crimes, even though some of the travelers who'd been killed were known to have carried small sums of money.[45]

Large crowds of curious onlookers gathered on the grounds of the Bender place as the bodies were still being uncovered, and they remained over the next few days as the tedious process of searching for additional victims continued. On Thursday, May 8, a crowd estimated at more than one thousand people milled around.[46]

The story of the Bender murders made front-page news across the country, from St. Louis to New York City. Headlines in the *Chicago Tribune* referred to the "diabolical crimes of the Bender gang" as "the Kansas Butchery."[47]

A number of people living in the vicinity of the Bender place were arrested shortly after the bodies were discovered on suspicion of being in cahoots with the murderous crew or of knowing something about the family's current whereabouts. One of the Benders' near neighbors, Rudolph Brockman, for no better reason than the fact that he was German and seemed to be the Benders' closest acquaintance, was taken from his home, strung up to a tree several miles away, and almost choked to death in an effort to get him to tell what he might know about the murders. When Brockman still insisted that he knew nothing about the crimes or the whereabouts of the Benders, he was finally let go.[48]

After the bodies were found, a number of people came forward with sensational stories about the murderous Bender clan. One woman told of the time she left a side saddle at the Bender house as collateral for Kate's medicinal services. When the treatment proved unsuccessful and the woman returned to retrieve the saddle, she was forced to participate in a strange ritual involving a series of incantations and a "spiritualistic manual of arms" during which the family members drew a large butcher knife across their throats and made "other significant motions." The woman slipped out during a lull in the séance and, upon being discovered, barely escaped from the Benders with her life. A man told of the time he'd stopped at the Bender place and, while seated, saw a man approach him from behind with a hammer. Drawing his pistol, he whirled on the man, who adroitly pretended to be driving a nail. As one newspaper observed, so many people came forward with strange stories like this that it seemed "almost wonderful that these occurrences [had] not long ago directed suspicion" toward the Benders.[49]

Speculation also abounded about the makeup of the Bender family. One report claimed the old man's given name was William, and another suggested that young John Bender's real surname was Gebhardt. Several newspapers claimed that Kate and young John Bender were not actual siblings but were instead both products of previous marriages. Some people even said that Kate and her supposed brother lived in sin as man and wife. Several reports agreed that Kate was good looking, although others claimed her features were very severe. Almost all reports gave Kate's age as early to mid-twenties. In truth, she was only sixteen, and much of the other speculation was likely nonsense as well. The best evidence is that the Benders were a traditional family, just as they represented themselves to Brockman and other neighbors, although Kate may have had other older siblings who had died.[50]

Investigation in the wake of the discovery of the bodies revealed that the Benders had absconded from their home within a few days after Senator York's visit on April 2. Posses were organized to try to hunt the fugitives down, and Governor Osborn offered a $500 reward for their capture. They were tracked to Thayer, where they'd abandoned their wagon and team on April 6 and taken a train to Chanute. From there, it was thought they might have boarded a southbound train and made their way to Texas, but they'd had a month's head start. No further sign of them was ever found for sure.[51]

False sightings of the Benders were rampant in the aftermath of their crimes. They were supposedly spotted in Texas, for example, in November 1873, and such dubious sightings continued for the next thirty years. In late 1889, two women accused of being Kate Bender and her mother were even arrested in Michigan and brought back to Kansas to face charges. They were finally released in April 1890 when it was decided they were not the Bender women.[52]

Within two or three years after the Bender murders, stories began to appear claiming that the reason all the reported sightings of the Benders turned out to be phony was that vigilantes had overtaken and killed the villainous family in Indian Territory soon after the bodies of their victims were discovered. Into the 1880s and beyond, men continued to come forward claiming to have been members of the vigilante posse that overtook the Benders and dispatched them to hell.[53]

The story that the Benders had been overtaken and killed shortly after the murders were discovered contained several flaws. The Benders had a head start of a whole month. It seems hardly plausible that they would have lingered in the area, allowing themselves to be overtaken only thirty or forty miles from the scene of their crimes. Senator York, Governor Osborn, and

# GOVERNOR'S PROCLAMATION.

# $2,000 REWARD

### State of Kansas, Executive Department.

WHEREAS, several atrocious murders have been recently committed in Labette County, Kansas, under circumstances which fasten, beyond doubt, the commissions of these crimes upon a family known as the "Bender family," consisting of

JOHN BENDER, about 60 years of age, five feet eight or nine inches in height, German, speaks but little English, dark complexion, no whiskers, and sparely built;

MRS. BENDER, about 50 years of age, rather heavy set, blue eyes, brown hair, German, speaks broken English;

JOHN BENDER, Jr., alias John Gebardt, five feet eight or nine inches in height, slightly built, gray eyes with brownish tint, brown hair, light moustache, no whiskers, about 27 years of age, speaks English with German accent;

KATE BENDER, about 24 years of age, dark hair and eyes, good looking, well formed, rather bold in appearance, fluent talker, speaks good English with very little German accent:

AND WHEREAS, said persons are at large and fugitives from justice, now therefore, I, Thomas A. Osborn, Governor of the State of Kansas, in pursuance of law, do hereby offer a REWARD OF FIVE HUNDRED DOLLARS for the apprehension and delivery to the Sheriff of Labette County, Kansas, of each of the persons above named.

In Testimony Whereof, I have hereunto subscribed my name, and caused the Great Seal of the State to be affixed.

[L. S.]       Done at Topeka, this 17th day of May, 1873.

### THOMAS A. OSBORN,
Governor.

By the Governor:
W. H. SMALLWOOD,
Secretary of State.

*Left*: Governor's proclamation offering reward for the Benders. *Author's collection.*

*Below*: Historical marker about the Benders at intersection of U.S. 169 and U.S. 400. *Photo by the author.*

other people in the best position to know discounted the vigilante stories as "sensational and fabulous." If vigilantes had, in fact, overtaken the Benders and killed them, why did the avengers wait several years before coming forward to reveal themselves? They had no reason to do so, because they had nothing to fear from the law. If they had made the death of the Benders known at the time it happened, they not only would have collected a sizeable reward but also would have been greeted as heroes. In addition, the stories of the various men who came forward to claim they were members of the vigilante posse were inconsistent in the details of how the fugitives were overtaken and killed.[54]

As a current Kansas historical marker near the site of the old Bender place aptly states, the disappearance of the Benders "remains one of the great unsolved mysteries of the old West."

# 4

# THE "ROWDY JOE" LOWE
# AND "RED" BEARD SHOWDOWN

## TWO SALOONKEEPERS SHOOT IT OUT

I n October 1872, a Topeka newspaper correspondent visited the booming
cattle town of Wichita and reported that it was the "liveliest and fastest
town" he'd seen in Kansas since "the days of '57," a reference to the pre–
Civil War border troubles. Among the places the newsman visited was the
dance hall and saloon of Joseph "Rowdy Joe" Lowe, located on the west side
of the Arkansas River in the lawless town of Delano (now part of Wichita).
Raucous cowboys frequented the place looking to be entertained by the
"painted and jeweled courtesans" who worked at the establishment, but Joe,
acting as "his own policeman," maintained "the best of order," according to
the correspondent. "No one is disposed to pick a quarrel with him."[55]

But that was about to change.

Not long after the Topeka newspaperman's visit, Edward T. "Red" Beard
appeared on the scene and started building his own dance hall just thirty
feet away from Rowdy Joe's. Things went smoothly at first, but a rivalry
gradually developed and finally erupted into violence in the fall of 1873.
Considering the reputations of both men, it was bound to happen.[56]

Joseph Lowe grew up in Illinois and came west as a young man. By the
time he landed in the cattle town of Ellsworth, Kansas, in the late 1860s,
he'd already earned the moniker "Rowdy Joe" for his boisterous behavior
and tough persona. Somewhere along the line, he met a woman named
Kate and took her as his wife or mistress, and she soon became known as
"Rowdy Kate," because of her association with Joe. In Ellsworth, twenty-
four-year-old Joe was a saloonkeeper, and he and Kate also ran a house of ill

Joseph "Rowdy Joe" Lowe. *Kansas State Historical Society.*

repute. After several scrapes with the law in Ellsworth, Joe and Kate left for the new cow town of Newton.[57]

Rowdy Joe reached Newton and resumed the saloon business in the summer of 1871, several weeks before the infamous Hide Park gunfight at a rival establishment in August of that year. A month later, Joe's dance hall staged its own deadly shootout when a Texan opened fire on the assistant city marshal, killing him and mortally wounding a local grocer. Then, in mid-February 1872, Joe killed a man named Sweet in a dispute over Rowdy Kate. He was acquitted at his preliminary examination on a plea of self-defense. In early June 1872, he and Kate packed up and moved again, this time to Wichita, where the railroad's arrival had turned the place into a cattle boomtown.[58]

Edward T. Beard, known as "Red" because of his red hair, was also from Illinois. He came from a prominent family after whom Beardstown, Illinois, was named, and he was considered a refined, educated person until after he and his wife got divorced. Leaving her and their three kids behind, Red went west about the time the Civil War ended and roamed throughout the western states, earning a reputation as a "terror to everybody." The forty-two-year-old Beard landed in Wichita in late 1872 or early 1873 and went into business across the river next to Rowdy Joe Lowe.[59]

The two coexisted on reasonably friendly terms at first, but Beard gradually came to resent Lowe's greater success and the reputation of his dance hall as the liveliest spot going. Beard's bitterness was likely aggravated by an incident that happened at his place in June 1873 and the repercussions that followed. In the wee hours of Tuesday morning, June 3, "a party of rowdies" and a squad of soldiers from the Sixth U.S. Cavalry got into a shooting affray over some of Red's girls, resulting in serious injuries to two soldiers and one of the girls, Emma Stanley. Late Wednesday night, the soldiers came back and burned Red's place to the ground, but Rowdy Joe's was saved when the fire threatened to spread to his dance hall. Red rebuilt and was back in business by August, but in the intervening two months, Rowdy Joe had a virtual monopoly on the cowboys' patronage.[60]

Red's mounting hostility toward Rowdy Joe came to a head on the night of October 27, 1873. Red got raving drunk and started shooting up his own place, blasting away at a doorknob at one point. He then went to the window that faced Rowdy Joe's dance hall and fired a pistol shot across the space separating the two buildings and through the window of Joe's place.[61]

Within a few minutes, Joe came stomping into Red's place with a shotgun, demanding to know who the S.O.B. was who shot at him. When Red owned up to the deed, he and Joe immediately exchanged shots. Joe was grazed in the neck but not seriously wounded, while his own shot went astray and struck a customer named Billie Anderson in the head, blinding him for life. Joe and Red tried to shoot a couple of more times, but their guns misfired.[62]

Rowdy Kate came in behind Joe, and Red snapped his pistol at her, too, before she managed to herd Joe out of the building. Red left by a different door but soon stormed back in looking for his shotgun. He accused his mistress, Josephine "Jo" DeMerritt, of double-crossing him and momentarily directed his wrath at her. Walter Beebe, Red's bartender, helped restrain Red until Jo made her escape and took refuge at Rowdy Joe's place. As soon as Beebe and the other men holding Red let him go, he went after Jo with pistol in hand. Entering the dim light of Rowdy Joe's establishment, he fired at the first woman he saw, Annie Franklin, perhaps mistaking her for Jo. Annie, one of Rowdy's dance girls, received a serious wound to the abdomen but eventually recovered.[63]

Enraged that Red had tried to kill both him and Kate, Rowdy Joe was not ready to let the melee end. After getting his wound dressed and reloading his shotgun, he stepped back into the night looking for Beard. As Beard started across the bridge separating Delano and Wichita, Joe shot him from ambush, seriously wounding him in the arm and hip.[64]

Rowdy Joe promptly turned himself in and was released on $2,000 bond. Red Beard lingered for about two weeks before dying on November 11, 1873, from infection caused by his wounds. His dance hall continued humming along, though, under the management of Jo DeMerritt.[65]

Pleading self-defense, Lowe was acquitted on December 11 in the death of Red Beard. He was immediately re-arrested for his assault on Billie Anderson, but a few days later, he escaped from his guard with the aid of Rowdy Kate, Walter Beebe, and others. Beebe, Red's former bartender, was later sent to the penitentiary on a charge of aiding a prisoner to escape. Sedgwick County sheriff William Smith offered a reward of $100 for the apprehension of Rowdy Joe, who was described as "5 feet 9 inches tall, heavy set, dark complexion, black hair, and heavy black moustache, gruff manners."[66]

The city of Wichita, though, was mostly just glad to be rid of Joe Lowe and his ilk. On January 8, 1874, the *Wichita Eagle* crowed that the town was "fast getting rid of that element which has proved such a curse to her prosperity." Red Beard was dead, Rowdy Joe had skipped bail, and Rowdy Kate had left "for parts unknown." Beebe was in the Kansas State Penitentiary, and Jo DeMerritt had joined him there, sent up on a forgery conviction.[67]

Meanwhile, Rowdy Joe made his way to St. Louis, where he registered at the Laclede Hotel under an assumed name, A.A. Becker. He was arrested there in early January 1874 by a St. Louis detective and held for Sheriff Smith, but Rowdy Kate reached St. Louis ahead of Smith and was allowed to hire a lawyer with money that Lowe had in his possession when he was arrested. The lawyer filed a writ of habeas corpus, and Rowdy Joe was released before Smith could arrive. Joe and Kate fled to Texas, where they finally split a couple of years later. Rowdy Joe remarried and moved to Colorado, where he was killed by an ex-policeman in a Denver saloon in 1899. Kate remained in Texas as a bawdy house madam at least into the 1880s. What eventually happened to her is uncertain, although one report claimed she died at San Angelo.[68]

# THE BLACK MASKERS OF COWLEY COUNTY

## THE KILLING OF SHERIFF SHENNEMAN
## AND LYNCHING OF CHARLES COBB

After killing a lawman about thirty miles northeast of Topeka, Kansas, in early January 1883, nineteen-year-old Charley Cobb fled the area and was last spotted heading south. Located in Cowley County later the same month, Cobb once again shot and killed the lawman who went out to arrest him, but this time he was apprehended before he could take flight. Outraged by the murder of their sheriff, the vigilantes of Cowley County made sure Cobb never got a chance to kill again.[69]

On the night of Friday, January 5, 1883, a local literary society held a meeting at the Pacific School in rural Jefferson County a few miles southeast of Valley Falls, Kansas, and Charley Cobb showed up looking to make trouble. Cobb was a "wayward, ungovernable" youth who'd run away to Texas about two years earlier and had just returned home a couple of months earlier, bragging about the wild life he'd led in the Lone Star State. After the meeting adjourned, he accosted Henry McClenny, head of the literary society, who was driving a wagon a short distance from the schoolhouse with several female passengers aboard. The two young men argued, and Cobb ended up firing several shots over the heads of the passengers.[70]

The next morning, a warrant for Charley Cobb's arrest on a charge of disorderly conduct was placed in the hands of Valley Falls constable Daniel Weiser, and he and his son Robert promptly set out to serve it. They found Cobb at his father's farm about five miles southeast of town, but young Cobb refused to surrender. When he secured a rifle and began maneuvering as though to offer a stiff resistance, the elder Weiser, who'd already gained a reputation as a "quick shooter" for the killing of a man during an arrest attempt a few months earlier, rashly opened fire, wounding Charley's thirteen-year-old brother, William. Enraged at seeing his brother shot, Charley returned fire, killing Dan Weiser and wounding his son.[71]

Charley Cobb fled the scene and was spotted in Chase County southwest of Topeka a few days after the shooting. Continuing southwest, he was seen near El Dorado in Butler County on January 11. He was still headed in a generally southerly or southwesterly direction, toward Cowley County, and the sheriff there, Albert T. Shenneman, was telegraphed to be on the lookout for the fugitive.[72]

On January 15, Cobb stopped at the farm of Walter and Ruth Jacobus, in Maple Township in the northwest corner of Cowley County, and asked for work. Giving his name as George Smith, he told the couple that he was a cowboy just up from Texas on his way home to Pennsylvania and that he needed work until spring, when he planned to continue the journey. When the couple told the young man they had no work for him, he offered to pay his board if he could stay with them for a week while he looked for work, and Mr. and Mrs. Jacobus finally accepted him on those terms.[73]

All went smoothly for the next week. The couple thought it a little strange that "Smith" always kept his revolver close by, even sleeping with it under his pillow, but they passed the behavior off as just part of "his cowboy ways." At the end of the week, Walter and Ruth decided to hire the young man after all, and they let him stay on as a farmhand. In the meantime, however, Sheriff Shenneman had learned through a rural schoolmaster who boarded with the Jacobus family of the stranger's presence on the Jacobus farm. Suspecting that the young man might be the fugitive from Jefferson County, Shenneman went out from Winfield on the morning of Tuesday, January 23 to investigate and to make an arrest if necessary.[74]

The Jacobus couple and their new hired hand were eating their noon meal when Shenneman drove up in a buggy and called Mr. Jacobus outside. The sheriff concocted a scheme to get inside the house without arousing suspicion, and Jacobus agreed to go along. Taking the sheriff inside, Jacobus introduced him as Dr. Jones of nearby Udall. As Shenneman passed through the kitchen into an adjoining room, he closely scrutinized the young man seated at the dinner table and decided that he was almost certainly the wanted fugitive. About this time, Cobb rose from the table and started toward the door. Sheriff Shenneman sprang on him from behind, trying to disarm him, but Cobb, who was stronger than his small frame suggested, broke away enough to get off two shots that struck the sheriff in the stomach.[75]

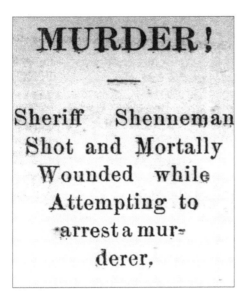

# MURDER!

---

Sheriff Shenneman Shot and Mortally Wounded while Attempting to arrest a murderer.

Headline describing the murder of Sheriff Shenneman. *From the* Arkansas City (KS) Arkansas Valley Democrat.

With the wounded man still hanging on to Cobb, Walter Jacobus, who was right behind the sheriff, rushed in and got the pistol away. Jacobus ordered Cobb to surrender or he'd kill him, and the young man promptly obeyed, crying out that he gave up and for Jacobus not to shoot him.[76]

Meanwhile, the sheriff released his grip on Cobb. "Hold him, he has killed me," Shenneman said, as he staggered away and slumped onto a nearby bed.

Jacobus sent his wife to the school where their boarder taught, and the schoolmaster hurried to the Jacobus home to tie up and help guard the prisoner until other neighbors arrived as reinforcements.[77]

Word reached Winfield, about twenty miles away, at two o'clock in the afternoon that Sheriff Shenneman had been shot, perhaps fatally, and a number of townspeople, including a reporter for the *Winfield Courier*, hurried out to the scene. The reporter and his party found almost the entire neighborhood gathered at the Jacobus home. Many of the neighbors were helping guard the prisoner in one room, while the gravely wounded sheriff lay in bed in an adjoining room, attended by two physicians.[78]

Despite his serious injuries, the thirty-six-year-old Shenneman was still able to talk to the reporter. He explained that he hadn't pulled his revolver on Cobb because he hated to pull a weapon on such a mere lad. He thought he'd be able to grab the boy and hold him while Jacobus disarmed him, but the wiry Cobb proved to be "a regular Hercules in strength."[79]

The doctors who attended Shenneman decided his condition was too serious for him to be moved, and the patient remained at the Jacobus residence. Privately, the doctors told the reporter they thought the sheriff had less than a one in ten chance of recovery.[80]

Acting on Shenneman's orders, Crowley County deputies George McIntire and A.B. Taylor started with the prisoner to Winfield in the sheriff's buggy. Meanwhile, the reporter and the rest of his party caught a train at Udall and came back to Winfield by rail. A large number of would-be vigilantes were at the depot when the train arrived, expecting the prisoner to be on board. They made a rush toward the passenger coach when it pulled to a halt and were reluctant to believe that Cobb was not among the passengers. Finally convinced, they scattered throughout the town, watching the jail and all the roads leading to it.[81]

Late that night, Deputies McIntire and Taylor sneaked Cobb into town, using a roundabout route, and hid him in a woodshed, where McIntire guarded him until the mob finally began to disperse after midnight. Later, the deputies took the prisoner to the county jail, where a *Courier* reporter found him "crouched in a corner" after daylight on Wednesday morning, January 24.[82]

The newspaperman observed that the prisoner's physical appearance tallied with the description that had been telegraphed to Sheriff Shenneman a week earlier: "about nineteen or twenty years old; light complexion; no whiskers or mustache; blue eyes; a scar over eye or cheek, don't know which; height five to five feet three inches; weight 125 to 130 pounds."[83]

The reporter added that the prisoner looked to be "a bright, healthy, smooth-faced boy" with "but few of the characteristics of a desperado. He is a perfect picture of robust health, muscular and compact as an athlete.... In talking, he uses excellent language, speaks grammatically and shows evidence of good breeding."[84]

Sticking to the same story he'd told Mr. and Mrs. Jacobus, Cobb informed the *Courier* man that his name was George Smith, that he'd recently arrived in Kansas from Texas, and that his home was in Pennsylvania. Relating how Sheriff Shenneman had been introduced to him as a doctor, Cobb said he immediately thought, when the so-called doctor jumped him, that he and Jacobus had conspired to rob him, since he was carrying about fifty dollars he'd been paid for his cowboy work. The prisoner claimed that if the sheriff had properly identified himself and drew his gun on him instead of physically attacking him, he would not have resisted. Cobb said the only thing he was guilty of was defending himself.[85]

The newspaperman concluded that, although the prisoner claimed not to be Charley Cobb, he was almost certainly lying, since his physical description matched so well that of the Jefferson County desperado, including the scar above his eye.[86]

In anticipation of possible mob action, especially if the sheriff were to die, local authorities decided not to risk leaving the prisoner at the Cowley County Jail. On the afternoon of January 24, Deputy Frank Finch escorted Cobb by train to Wichita, where he was lodged in the Sedgwick County Jail.[87]

Shenneman lingered in agony at the Jacobus home until Thursday night, January 25. He died at about 9:45 p.m. with his wife, a brother, several fellow law officers, and a number of other friends by his side.[88]

On Friday, the sheriff of Jefferson County arrived in Wichita escorting one of Cobb's neighbors, who positively identified the prisoner as Charles Cobb, the same man who'd killed Constable Weiser. Later the same day, however, when a *Wichita Daily Times* reporter visited the prisoner at the jail, Cobb still maintained that his name was George Smith. He said the Jefferson County man had obviously lied, because he'd never seen the man before.[89]

The *Times* newsman described Cobb's physical appearance in terms similar to those of the *Courier* reporter, except the Wichita reporter thought the prisoner weighed closer to 150 pounds than 130. Like the Winfield newspaperman, the *Times* reporter noted Cobb's muscular build, adding that he appeared to be solid muscle; but unlike the *Courier* scribe, who thought Cobb had few characteristics of a desperado, the Wichita writer said the prisoner's face revealed a "bold unabashed, cruel blood desire." His wedge shape and pointed chin gave him a wolf-like appearance, although he was not repulsive but rather the reverse, with his "shapely nose and mouth" and clear complexion.[90]

Although disinclined to talk, Cobb finally repeated the same story he'd told the other newspaperman, claiming he was from Pennsylvania. He refused to say what town he was from, however, because he did not want his folks to know the trouble he was in. He repeated that, if the sheriff had announced himself as a lawman instead of trying to jump him, he would have surrendered peaceably.[91]

On Saturday morning, January 27, Deputy Taylor, Sheriff Joseph M. Thralls of Sumner County, and Sheriff H.R. Watt of Sedgwick County started with Cobb overland in a carriage from Wichita to Winfield for preliminary examination. When the citizens of Winfield got word of the prisoner's pending arrival, a mob of men formed with the intention of taking him from the lawmen. When the officers reached the outskirts of Winfield late that night, Taylor left Cobb in the hands of the two sheriffs while he went to scout out the situation in town. Reporting back that it would be "certain death" for Cobb if they attempted to lodge him in the county jail, Taylor took over the team and carriage while the sheriffs escorted the prisoner away from town on foot. Shortly afterward, a squad of vigilantes intercepted Taylor, and, according to the *Winfield Courier*, "men came running wild with excitement" from all parts of town, crowding around the deputy and demanding to know where Cobb was. "As the crowd surged to and fro, it seemed as if the very air was ladened with cries of vengeance." The wild scene, according to the *Courier*, defied description.[92]

For a while, it looked as if Taylor was going to be "roughly treated," and he was compelled to tell where he had left the sheriffs and the prisoner. The mob forced the deputy to show them the exact spot, and the maddened horde spent the rest of the night vainly scouring the neighborhood, searching sheds and other possible hiding places. Meanwhile, in the wee hours of Sunday morning, the sheriffs secured another carriage a few miles outside of town, and Sheriff Watt escorted the prisoner back to Wichita, while Sheriff Thralls returned to Winfield.[93]

Sheriff Shenneman's funeral service and burial were held on Sunday, January 28. One of the preachers who spoke likened the human desire for vengeance to a higher law demanding that each person should suffer for his sins, but he went on to urge the people of Winfield to emulate their dead sheriff, who always sought to protect even the most hardened prisoners from violence, by letting the law take its course.[94]

On Wednesday, January 31, Deputy Taylor again brought Cobb from Wichita to Winfield, and the prisoner was successfully lodged in the Cowley County Jail early that evening.

But he didn't stay long.

Shortly after Cobb was placed in jail, Ella Shenneman, the sheriff's widow, went to see him. According to the *Courier*, when she looked into his eyes "with her face bathed in tears, the prisoner broke down completely and wept like a child." A number of other citizens were also allowed to see the prisoner during the evening. About 11:00 p.m., he asked to see Mrs. Shenneman again, and when she returned to the jail, he confessed to her that he was, in fact, Charles Cobb, and he asked her to write to Dan Weiser's wife in Jefferson County and tell her he was sorry for having killed the constable.[95]

By 2:00 a.m. on the morning of February 1, all had settled down at the jail, and only a few pedestrians remained on the streets. But about 2:30, an organized squad of thirteen men wearing black masks came marching down Ninth Avenue to the courthouse grounds located at Ninth and Fuller. They filed onto the grounds and gained entrance to the sheriff's office in front of the jail. They covered George McIntire, who'd taken over as sheriff, with their revolvers and forced him, under threat of having his head blown off, to hand over the keys to the jail. Three or four of "the black maskers," said the *Courier*, went into the jail and soon came out with the prisoner between them."[96]

The mob herded the prisoner west on Ninth to Main Street, north one block to Eighth and then west on Eighth to a railroad bridge over the Walnut River at the edge of town. The commotion at the jail aroused the townspeople, and a number of curious onlookers followed the procession toward the bridge. Two of the vigilantes dropped back with drawn revolvers and ordered the spectators to keep their distance, but several boys crept up in the brush along the riverbank and got close to the bridge, where they could see what happened.[97]

Someone among the mob produced a rope and tied one end of it to a beam of the bridge, while the other end, which had already been looped with a noose, was placed around Cobb's neck. The leader of the gang told the prisoner in a gruff voice that, if he had anything to say, to say it quick. "Oh, don't, boys!" Cobb cried. "Father have mercy on me!"[98]

Positioning the doomed man on the bridge, the vigilantes dropped him between the railings to his death. He fell about ten feet and rebounded about half that distance. Most of the mob then filed on across the bridge, while two of their number remained on guard until the main body got across. As soon as the guards followed the other lynchers, the curious onlookers surged up to the bridge to gawk at the suspended man.[99]

The body was cut down about daylight on the morning of February 1, and Coroner H.L. Wells convened an inquest that continued into the next day. After hearing testimony from Sheriff McIntire, Deputy Taylor, and several other witnesses, about the only relevant factor the jury learned was that the leader of the mob spoke with a deep, gruff voice. The jury, therefore, concluded that Charles Cobb had come to his death at the hands of parties unknown.[100]

On Friday, February 2, Coroner Wells received a telegram from Cobb's father asking that his son's body be sent home to Jefferson County for burial, and after the inquest concluded later that day, the body was accordingly boxed up and shipped by rail to Mr. Cobb.[101]

Editorial opinion about the mob action that claimed Cobb's life was divided. For example, the *Wichita Eagle*, calling Cobb a "hapless boy," suggested that he was at least partly a victim of unfortunate circumstances. The commentator reminded readers that Cobb's younger brother had been needlessly shot before Cobb mortally wounded Constable Weiser. The *Eagle* also questioned why Cobb was taken back to Cowley County from Wichita so soon after Shenneman's death when everybody knew that mob fever was running high in Winfield.[102]

The *Wichita Daily Times* took an opposite view. Suggesting that Cobb was a hardened desperado who got what he deserved, the *Times* repeated a rumor that Cobb had boasted to Deputy Taylor during his ride back to Winfield that he'd killed at least one other man besides Weiser and Shenneman and that he meant to kill several others, including Deputy Taylor himself, if he ever got a chance.[103]

The *Winfield Courier* was noticeably mum on the righteousness of the mob action until a local man, J.B. Evans, wrote to the newspaper demanding that it take a stand. Evans himself felt, like the *Wichita Eagle*, that law officers had not done enough to protect Cobb, even hinting that they'd deliberately been lax in their security because they secretly wanted him to hang. Evans also thought the minister who preached Shenneman's funeral service should have condemned mob action in stronger terms.[104]

Accusing Evans of not having all the facts, the *Courier* in rebuttal strongly defended the deputies and other officers charged with safeguarding Cobb. While not condoning mob action in general, the newspaperman claimed the vigilantes were justified in this instance, if any extralegal action could ever be justified, because the *Courier* man, like the *Wichita Daily Times* commentator, considered Cobb a desperado and wannabe Jesse James. The *Courier* also pointed out that the minister who'd preached the sheriff's funeral had indeed urged his listeners to let the law take its course and not to resort to mob action.[105]

# 6

# GUNFIGHT AT HUNNEWELL

## THE SHOOTIN'EST TOWN IN KANSAS

After a deadly gunfight at Hunnewell, Kansas, on the night of August 12, 1884, the initial report of the incident wired to newspapers across the state was skimpy on details. The shooting was the result of "an old feud" and had left the town's deputy marshal gravely wounded, but most of the other particulars could not be learned. Later accounts suggest that the "old feud" might not have been very old, but it's difficult, even today, to piece together exactly what happened. Suffice it to say, there was more to the story than what was contained in the first report.[106]

Hunnewell, located in southern Sumner County on the Oklahoma border, was one of many cow towns that sprang up in Kansas during the years after the Civil War, as Texas cattlemen started driving their herds to railroad shipping points in the Sunflower State. As a railhead of the Leavenworth, Lawrence and Galveston Railway, Hunnewell pulsed with rowdy activity, especially during cattle season, with the town catering to the cowboys. Harry French, conductor on the LL&G, recalled that Hunnewell had one hotel, two stores, one barbershop, a couple of dance halls, and eight or nine saloons in the early 1880s.[107]

It was like "Dodge City on a smaller scale," French said, except there was "no Bat Masterson to control the casual use of firearms, and there was more shooting than I ever saw in Dodge City."[108]

Emboldened by the proximity of Indian Territory, the cowboys of Hunnewell "more than lived up to their reputation as hell-raisers," because they knew they could retreat into the territory and would not be pursued by lawmen. French said Hunnewell was "the shootin'est town" he ever saw: "It was not uncommon for a group of whiskey-mad cowboys to take a violent dislike to some particular saloon or store. They would mount their ponies, shoot up the town, and ride their horses full tilt into the offending saloon or place of business. The cowboys owned the town. They knocked the heads off sugar barrels so that the ponies might eat their fill. Guns blazed day and night."[109]

Into this bedlam came twenty-three-year-old Hamilton Rayner, hired as chief deputy by Hunnewell city marshal Joe Forsythe in 1883, to help bring law and order to the town. When Forsythe resigned in frustration in December of that year over what he saw as the city fathers' lax attitude toward the cowboys, Rayner took over as marshal. He recruited another young man, former Texas Ranger Ed Scotten, as his own chief deputy.[110]

Somewhere along the line, Marshal Rayner grew infatuated with a pretty, black-haired girl who worked at Pat Hanly's saloon. According to a cowboy who was acquainted with her, "She was a peach, but hardly the kind to be a Sunday school teacher or lead a prayer meeting."[111]

A rival for her affections appeared on the scene in August 1884 in the person of Oscar Halsell. A twenty-five-year-old cowboy turned cattleman, Halsell was camped on the Chikaskia River in Indian Territory just south of Hunnewell with a herd of cattle that his friend Clem Barefoot had charge of. Barefoot, Halsell, and their hands spent their free time in town, carousing and having a good time. Halsell was drawn to the pretty girl in Pat Hanly's saloon, and she favored him with her attention as well—too much to suit Marshal Rayner.[112]

On Saturday, August 9, Barefoot, Halsell, and some of their boys came into Hunnewell and, "after making the rounds of the saloons and filling up with devil juice," according to a contemporaneous newspaper report, "began their usual drunken pastime of promiscuous shooting." Marshal Rayner, who had a reputation for being rough on cowboys, got after them, but they escaped back to the territory.[113]

The following Tuesday night, August 12, the cowboys came back and went to Hanly's saloon, where they made some "noisy demonstrations." Marshal Rayner and Deputy Scotten went to the saloon and ordered them to quiet down. Saying they'd come to have a good time, the cowboys challenged the marshals to a fight. When the lawmen replied that they didn't want to fight unless they had to, the cowboys invited them to stay for a drink. Accepting the offer, the marshals took a quick drink and then left. Barefoot and Halsell followed them outside and, according to the *Caldwell Advance*, immediately started shooting. In the initial barrage, Scotten collapsed with a bullet to the

It's unknown whether this mock hanging in Hunnewell in August 1884 was related to the gunfight that occurred there the same month, but it seems likely. *Kansas State Historical Society.*

neck, while Rayner received a flesh wound near the knee. He managed to return fire, though, aiming for Barefoot. Halsell and Barefoot fled on foot, but Rayner thought his shot had taken effect. A cowboy who'd been in the saloon with Barefoot and Halsell was arrested, although he had taken no part in the shootout.[114]

Doctors who examined Scotten in the aftermath of the gunfight found that the deadly bullet had barely missed his jugular vein but had injured his spinal cord, paralyzing him from the neck down. Doctors held out little hope that he would survive. Meanwhile, Barefoot and Halsell made their way south to their camp on the Chikaskia, where they secured horses and continued south before parting ways at daylight the next morning.[115]

Attempting to assign a cause for the Hunnewell gunfight, initial reports could say only that it was the result of "an old feud" between Rayner and Barefoot. Later accounts, however, seem to indicate that the argument was between Rayner and Halsell, that the pretty saloon girl was the object of the feud, and that the dispute wasn't particularly old. Initial reports also tended to assign complete blame for the incident to the rowdy cowboys, but later statements suggest that the fault wasn't as clear-cut as the first newspaper stories implied. For instance, H.H. Halsell, in relating the gunfight many years later as told to him by his brother Oscar, claimed that the four participants in the shootout faced each other in a brief standoff outside the saloon before the firing began and that both sides commenced shooting about the same time. Halsell also said Marshal Rayner had been hounding his brother throughout the town, watching his every move.[116]

On August 19, one week after the gunfight, Governor George W. Glick issued a proclamation offering a reward of $100 for the arrest of Barefoot, Halsell, and two other cowboys charged with the murderous assault on the Hunnewell lawmen. The city of Hunnewell also offered a reward of $200 for their capture.[117]

After parting ways at daylight on the morning of August 13, Clem Barefoot and Oscar Halsell continued their flight south. With his horse nearly dead from exhaustion, Halsell reached his brother's camp deep in Indian Territory at midafternoon of the same day, having covered almost 100 miles in fifteen hours. Meanwhile, Barefoot, seriously injured from the gunshot wound Marshal Rayner had inflicted, made his slow way south, finally reaching his camp on the Washita River, 150 miles from Hunnewell, where he died the day after his arrival. The twenty-seven-year-old Barefoot had been employed for the previous three years by cattle contractors at the Wichita and Darlington Indian agencies, and the *Cheyenne Transporter*, published at the Darlington agency (near present-day El Reno, Oklahoma), eulogized him as "a quiet and peaceable man" who would "molest no one unless imposed upon."[118]

Deputy Scotten lingered in agony until September 2, when he died from the neck wound that had paralyzed him. His mother and brother were with him on his deathbed, and they took him back to his Texas home for burial.[119]

Oscar Halsell remained on the run for almost two years before finally turning himself in. Charges against him were dropped, and he went on to become a prominent rancher and businessman in Oklahoma. During the winter of 1890–91, he employed Bill Doolin, the future desperado, at his livery in Guthrie. Halsell died in 1922 at the age of sixty-two.[120]

Hamilton Rayner moved to New Orleans and later to El Paso, where he worked as a special railroad officer and also imported and bred Chihuahuas. He died in 1932 at the age of seventy-two.[121]

A number of circumstances, including the fact that railroads began extending into Texas, combined to end the cattle-drive era within a year or so after the Hunnewell gunfight. The town of Hunnewell quickly declined, although it managed to hang on to its post office until 1960. Today, its population is fewer than one hundred people.[122]

# 7
# FEMME FATALE MINNIE WALLACE WALKUP

## THE MOST FAMOUS MURDER TRIAL
## IN LYON COUNTY HISTORY

W hen J.R. Walkup, acting mayor of Emporia, Kansas, married a beautiful sixteen-year-old girl, Minnie Wallace, and brought her home as his bride on July 25, 1885, the newlyweds were greeted at the depot with congratulations and best wishes from many of Walkup's Emporia friends, and a reception was held in their honor later that evening. Local reporters and other observers remarked on the "personal attractions" and the "good qualities of mind and heart" of the youthful bride, and they ventured that she would make Walkup an excellent wife.[123]

But their opinion of the charming young lady would change in a hurry.

The forty-eight-year-old Walkup, whose second wife had died in May 1884, traveled to New Orleans in December of that year to take in the world's fair, and he stayed at the boardinghouse of Minnie's mother. He was immediately fascinated by the blossoming young woman; he'd been there only a day or two when he began wooing her.[124]

The daughter of a well-known New Orleans lawyer, Minnie was, according to a city newspaper, "a tall, graceful, slender, but well-developed girl, with perfect complexion, white, with the roses blooming on her cheeks blood red." Her long black hair, her "large black eyes and heavy eyelashes," and her "mastery of expression" completed the picture, which was "a rare one." Noted for her beauty at an early age, Minnie was educated at a prestigious New Orleans finishing school, and she had many admirers. The Wallace family was noted for the beauty of its female members, concluded the local paper, "and Miss Minnie was considered the fairest flower of the flock."[125]

After a short stay in New Orleans, Walkup went back to Emporia, but he returned two or three times during the next several months to attend the fair and to press his courtship of Minnie. The Wallace family also traveled to Emporia on at least one occasion, and the couple soon agreed to marry. On July 19, 1885, Walkup started east from Emporia on what was reported in the local press as "important business." He met the Wallaces in Covington, Kentucky, where the Wallace family had relatives, and he and Minnie were married there on July 22.[126]

Walkup brought his youthful bride home to Emporia three days later, and the couple settled into what seemed to be a happy honeymoon. About the first of August, Willie Willis, a cousin of Minnie's with whom she had grown up, arrived in Emporia to live with her and her new husband, and Walkup employed him in his office. On August 15, shortly after returning from a brief trip to Topeka, Walkup complained of feeling ill, and he grew sicker over the next couple of days. Doctors treated him for what they diagnosed as poisoning. Walkup died on Saturday morning, August 22, despite their efforts. Rumors started circulating around Emporia, even before Walkup's death, that he had been poisoned by his young bride. During his death struggle, Walkup showed symptoms of both strychnine and arsenic poisoning, and an informal investigation revealed that Minnie had purchased an unusual quantity of strychnine about the time Walkup took ill and had bought arsenic just a few days before he died.[127]

A coroner's inquest was called the same day Walkup died, but Willie Willis, who was a year or so older than Minnie, was arrested on suspicion even as a jury was being assembled, simply because he was considered "a profane youth." Several Emporia druggists testified at the inquest that Minnie Walkup had purchased or tried to purchase poison at their stores during the days leading up to her husband's death. One pharmacist said that, after Minnie came under suspicion, she asked him to come to her home and take back the arsenic she'd purchased from him. She wanted to show him that she had not used the poison, but as she was handing it over to him, she accidentally spilled it, and he was unable to tell whether all the arsenic he'd sold her was there or not. Walkup's unmarried daughter Libbie, who had helped with the care of her father, said she did not know of any poison on the Walkup premises, and J.R. Walkup himself, even as he realized he was suffering from poisoning of some sort, refused to suspect his wife. At least one witness said Walkup had told him he started feeling sick even before he left Topeka. When the jury adjourned without a verdict on Saturday night, Minnie, like her cousin, was taken into custody

Sketch of Minnie Wallace Walkup, twelve years after her murder trial in Emporia. *From the Chicago Tribune.*

to be held pending the outcome of the inquest, which was scheduled to resume on Monday.[128]

Minnie spent Sunday confined to her room and guarded by the sheriff and a deputy. Curious onlookers thronged around the house, and reporters called at the home to interview the prisoner. She spent much of the day sewing a dress she planned to wear to her late husband's funeral, but when the funeral took place the next day, she decided not to attend so as to avoid the whisperings and stares of a suspicious public. As the funeral cortege passed the house on its way to the cemetery, however, she stepped outside to greet the crowd. Although she did so at the suggestion of the sheriff, who hoped her appearance would satisfy the curiosity seekers and induce them to disperse, many observers criticized the gesture as a publicity-seeking stunt.[129]

The coroner's inquest continued throughout the week of August 24 and into the next. Despite all the unwanted attention directed at Minnie, she remained "cool and collected," and although the ordeal left her looking somewhat careworn, reporters continued to remark on her uncommon beauty. Staunchly maintaining her innocence, she conversed freely about the death of her husband and the ongoing inquest. The public was divided on the question of Minnie's guilt, but most of those who talked to her came away convinced that she was blameless. Minnie seemed to "exercise an influence over those brought into contact with her that is remarkable," observed the *Emporia Daily News*. "Men and women who have called upon her out of curiosity, believing her to be a criminal, have gone away regarding her as one of the most estimable and gentle ladies of the city."[130]

Unswayed by Minnie's personal charm, the coroner's jury returned a verdict on August 31 that J.R. Walkup had come to his death by arsenic poisoning at the hands of his wife, Minnie Walkup. Charged with murder, Minnie appeared for preliminary examination the next day, September 1, in a "neat black silk dress" and seemed "as calm and self-possessed as if making a morning call." The hearing, however, was postponed, and Minnie's attorney ultimately waived examination.[131]

Minnie's trial took place in late October in the Lyon County District Court at Emporia before Judge C.B. Graves. Large crowds attended each day, eager to get a glimpse of "the fair defendant, whose reputation for loveliness of face and figure" had "spread far and near." The state's theory of the crime was that Minnie was a gold digger who, in conspiracy with her mother and other Wallace family members, married Walkup only because she thought he was rich and that she killed him hoping to inherit his wealth. On rebuttal, the defense countered that Minnie had no motive for killing her husband, because she knew that his children from prior marriages were his primary beneficiaries. Minnie's lawyers admitted it was coincidental that she had purchased poison just before Walkup died, but even the most amateur of criminal minds would know better than to buy poison in the same small town where her victim lived just days before she planned to kill said victim. Minnie had, instead, bought the strychnine as a cleaning agent and the arsenic as a beauty aid for her complexion.[132]

Presenting its own theory of the case, the defense said Walkup's death was a result of his life of debauchery. He had suffered from syphilis and other diseases that contributed to his demise and had habitually dosed himself with arsenic over a number of years to enhance his sexual potency and to treat the syphilis. Thus, he had died from an accumulation of the poison in his system. Minnie's lawyers introduced witnesses who testified that Walkup had previously had attacks similar to, although not as severe as, that which brought on his death. Witnesses also testified that Walkup regularly frequented houses of ill fame, that they had seen him take arsenic on numerous occasions, and that he was already sick on his return trip from Topeka to Emporia in August 1885.[133]

The highlight of the trial came when Minnie took the stand in her own defense on October 29. She said her husband was sick when he came home from Topeka on Saturday afternoon, August 15, and that she summoned a doctor later that night despite his protestation that he had been sick like this before and would be all right without treatment. She said she bought the arsenic at his urging after he noticed a blotch on her face and she remarked that arsenic could get rid of it. Minnie said she remained by her husband's side throughout almost the entirety of his dying illness. Her testimony, observed one Emporia newspaper, was "very straightforward" and bore "the imprint of truth in every word." On cross-examination, Minnie bore up under the severe questioning with "almost unparalleled nerve."[134]

## A WONDERFUL WOMAN.

The Evidence in the Minnie Wallace Walkup Murder Case All Submitted.

Something About the Beautiful Young Woman and the Crime Charged to Her.

Her First Meeting With Mr. Walkup, the Brief Courtship and Marriage.

The Fair Prisoner Developing Traits That Stamp Her a Wonderful Woman.

Minnie won over many people to her side during her trial, as this headline suggests. *From the* St. Paul Globe.

On Friday afternoon, November 6, after fifty-two hours of deliberations, the jury in Minnie's case returned with a verdict of not guilty. The jurymen were reportedly initially split six for conviction and six for acquittal, but those for acquittal were so adamant that the other six were eventually won over. Minnie was reportedly overjoyed upon first learning of the outcome, but she received the official verdict with only the hint of a smile. That evening, she and a coterie of well-wishers gathered at a local residence to celebrate her newfound freedom, and Minnie entertained the guests by playing the piano.[135]

Some observers, of course, were unconvinced by the verdict. If not a cold-blooded murderer, they thought Minnie was, at the very least, a conceited, vampish girl who enjoyed the limelight her trial had shone on her, and they chastised those who fawned over Minnie and turned her into a celebrity.[136]

Future events would show that those who thought Minnie to be a vain, money-grabbing femme fatale might have been on the right track.

Minnie, her mother, and Willie Willis left Emporia for New Orleans on November 12. Minnie started going by her maiden name, Minnie Wallace, shortly after returning to New Orleans, although she claimed she only did so because people in her hometown knew her better by that name. Having inherited half of Walkup's estate, she frequently traveled with her mother to Europe and throughout the United States.[137]

William Pitt Kellogg, U.S. senator from Louisiana, soon became infatuated with Minnie, and he helped finance her move to Chicago in the early 1890s. In September 1897, she secretly married John B. Ketcham, a wealthy Chicago businessman who'd divorced his wife in favor of Minnie. In November 1897, less than two months after the marriage, Ketcham died under suspicious circumstances, but a coroner's investigation ruled that the death was the result of acute alcoholism.[138]

Ketcham willed his entire estate, worth about $250,000, to Minnie. However, Ketcham's brother and other relatives contested the will, and when the details of Minnie's previous marriage to Walkup were recalled, the case created a scandal that rivaled the one she had faced in Emporia more than ten years earlier. The two parties ultimately reached an agreement, allowing Minnie to inherit between $100,000 and $200,000.[139]

Then, in April 1914, an affair Minnie had been carrying on with millionaire capitalist D.H. Louderback came to light when the sixty-five-year-old Louderback died in Chicago and his will showed that he had bequeathed one-fourth of his wealth to his secret "friend," Mrs. Ketcham, as Minnie was now known. Although a coroner's inquest concluded that Louderback had died of cyanide poisoning, the death was ruled an accident. However, there remained "some mystery" about it, according to a Chicago newspaper. The revelation that Minnie was an heir to part of Louderback's fortune again revived stories of her Lucrezia Borgia–like past, with Kansas newspapers recounting, in particular, "the most famous murder trial ever held in Lyon County." But Minnie was never directly implicated in the poisoning of Louderback, since she was abroad at the time.[140]

Minnie died in San Diego, California, in 1957 at the age of eighty-eight.[141]

# 8

# A MOST TERRIFIC BATTLE

## THE DALTON GANG'S FIASCO AT COFFEYVILLE

Twenty-four-year-old Bob Dalton wanted to make a name for himself. Tired of living in the shadow of his more infamous kinfolk, he wanted to do something to set himself apart—something even Frank, Jesse, and Cousin Cole wouldn't have dreamed of. Like robbing two banks at the same time "just to show...it could be done." Wouldn't that be a laugh! Even the James-Younger gang in their glory days wouldn't have tried something so audacious. And what better place to pull it off than his old stomping grounds of Coffeyville, Kansas, where he knew the layout of the town and where almost nobody carried guns.[142]

But Bob Dalton didn't know Coffeyville and its citizens quite as well as he thought.

Bob and his brothers grew up in Missouri, south of Kansas City in the backyard of the Younger gang. Their mother, Adeline, was a half sister to Henry Washington Younger, father of Cole and his notorious brothers. Bob nursed a secret itch to be just like his celebrated cousins and their cohorts in crime, the James boys.[143]

After 1880, Adeline and her husband, Louis, moved the Dalton family to Kansas, and they lived at Coffeyville for two years during the late 1880s. One of the older sons, Frank, was killed in Indian Territory (Oklahoma) in late 1887 while serving as a deputy U.S. marshal. Bob, older brother Grat, and younger brother Emmett followed Frank into the marshals service, but for the Daltons, as for a good number of Old West lawmen, the line between keeping the peace and breaking the law was a thin one. Bob killed a man named Montgomery in 1888 under the cover of authority, but the killing was widely criticized as unjustified. In mid-1890, the Dalton boys gave up marshaling altogether and moved to stealing horses.[144]

They soon graduated to train robbery, but now they had their sights set on something even bigger. Shortly after 9:30 on Wednesday morning, October 5, 1892, Bob, Grat, Emmett, and two other gang members, Richard "Dick" Broadwell and Bill Power, came riding boldly into Coffeyville from the west "at a swinging trot." Leaving clouds of dust in their wake as they thundered along Eighth Street, the horsemen were "armed to the teeth," and the Daltons wore false beards to hide their identities.[145]

Bob Dalton's big scheme started going awry as soon as the riders reached downtown Coffeyville. The hitching post on Eighth Street near the rear of the Condon Bank where the gang had planned to tie their horses had been taken up while the city made street improvements. Bob had reportedly been spotted in Coffeyville just a week earlier, but if he had indeed paid such a visit, he'd done a poor job of reconnoitering the place. The gang members were now forced to hitch their mounts to a fence at the far end of a narrow alley two blocks southwest of where they'd planned.[146]

Dismounting, the five outlaws marched east down the alley and emerged onto an open plaza that separated Walnut and Union Streets. A local man, Alec McKenna, recognized one of the Daltons, despite his disguise, and he watched the suspicious group as three of them crossed Walnut and walked through a front door of the Condon Bank while the other two headed across the plaza to the First National Bank on Union Street.[147]

McKenna saw one of the men who'd gone into the Condon point a Winchester toward a bank employee, and he immediately turned and yelled to a group of men in a nearby store that the bank was being robbed. The cry was taken up by others; soon, the whole plaza area was alerted. Men quickly armed themselves with weapons taken from local hardware stores, and they took up strategic positions surrounding the Condon.[148]

Inside the Condon, Grat Dalton and Dick Broadwell took positions commanding the two front entrances, while the third robber, Bill Power, located cashier C.M. Ball in an adjoining room and ordered him to fetch the money out of the safe. To try to placate the desperadoes, Ball dragged $4,000 from the vault, but he was not so willing to hand over the $40,000 inside the safe. Stalling for time, he announced that the safe was set on a time lock that would not open until 9:45. In fact, the timer had gone off at 8:00 a.m., but Power and the other robbers fell for the ruse, saying they would

*Left*: Modern-day photo of the Condon Bank building. *Below*: Historical marker about the Dalton raid on Coffeyville, embedded into the wall of the old Condon Bank building. *Photos by the author.*

EARLY SITE

C.M. CONDON & CO.

BANK

CONSTRUCTED IN 1890

ON OCTOBER 5, 1892, THE DALTON GANG RODE INTO COFFEYVILLE, KANSAS, TO ROB THE CONDON AND FIRST NATIONAL BANKS. FOLLOWING A 12-MINUTE GUN BATTLE FOUR MEMBERS OF THE DALTON GANG WERE KILLED - BOB & GRAT DALTON, BILL POWERS AND DICK BROADWELL. EMMETT DALTON SURVIVED. FOUR COURAGEOUS CITIZENS ALSO LAY DEAD - GEORGE CUBINE, CHARLES CONNELLY, CHARLES BROWN AND LUCIUS BALDWIN.

wait, since 9:45 was only three minutes away. They didn't even bother to check the door to the safe themselves.[149]

Meanwhile, Bob and Emmett Dalton entered the First National Bank and found a teller, the cashier, and one customer in the front room. Presenting their Winchesters, they called cashier Thomas Ayers by name, ordering him to hand over all the money in the bank. With one of the robbers keeping him covered, Ayers started collecting money from the tills and handing it over as unhurriedly as he dared, while the other robber went to a back room and herded a third employee, the bookkeeper, to the front. The desperadoes now ordered Ayers to get the money out of the vault, and he brought out a bundle containing about $5,000. At the same time, the robbers discovered a chest containing additional cash, and they stuffed it, along with the money from the tills and the vault, into a grain sack.[150]

Back at the Condon, just before the allotted three minutes expired, Dick Broadwell spotted some of the townspeople arming themselves and taking up strategic positions surrounding the bank. He fired a shot through the plate-glass front door of the bank toward a party of men positioned at Barndollar's store across the plaza on Union Street. Almost immediately, his shot was answered by a fusillade of gunfire crashing through the windows of the bank. One shot hit Broadwell in the arm, and he cried out that he'd been hit. Securing the money they'd already gathered, the three bandits started out the front doors with Grat Dalton in the lead, shooting his way out. As the men emerged onto the street, they came under heavy fire from Isham's Hardware Store, located next door to the First National, but they managed to run the gauntlet across the plaza to the alley, where their horses were tied.[151]

Inside the First National, Bob and Emmett Dalton, with their bagful of money, started to herd the three bankers out the front door just as the first shots rang out. Leaving cashier Ayers on the street, the robbers withdrew into the bank, where they turned the teller loose before exiting out the back door with the bookkeeper still in tow. They were met in the alley by Lucius Baldwin, a young man who had just stepped out the back door of Isham's Hardware with a pistol in his hand. Seeing the bookkeeper, Baldwin hesitated, and Bob Dalton shot him through the left breast just below the heart. As Baldwin fell to the ground mortally wounded, the Daltons abandoned their remaining hostage and hurried down the alley to Eighth Street, pursuing a circuitous route back to their horses. Emmett led the way carrying the money sack, while Bob wielded his Winchester in the rear.[152]

Heading west on Eighth, the two robbers paused at Union Street and saw George Cubine standing in front of Rammel's Drug Store guarding the front entrance of the First National Bank with a rifle in his hands. Bob took aim and shot Cubine dead with a bullet through his back and into his heart. An old citizen named Charles Brown picked up Cubine's weapon, and Bob promptly shot and killed him, too. Near the same place, the desperate Dalton spotted Cashier Ayers standing in front of Isham's Hardware Store with a rifle he'd procured from the store after escaping the robbers. Bob fired a shot that struck Ayers in the left cheek and passed out through his neck. The banker fell to the ground unconscious. The outlaws then raced down Eighth Street and turned south on an alley that intersected the east–west alley where the gang had left their horses. At the intersection of the two alleys, they met the other three members of the gang, who had fled from the Condon by the same route they'd approached it.[153]

By now, a number of citizens had procured arms and taken up positions commanding the alley, and they turned the narrow passageway into a shooting gallery as the robbers started toward their horses. "The firing was rapid and incessant for about three minutes," said the *Coffeyville Weekly Journal*.

Bob Dalton was the first man to fall, but he propped himself up against an old barn and fired several shots in the direction of Isham's Hardware before collapsing. His brother Grat was hit immediately afterward and fell beside Bob. Grat, too, pulled himself up against the barn. Marshal Charles Connelly and two or three other citizens entered the alley from the plaza in pursuit of the robbers. As soon as Connelly passed the fallen men, Grat, with great effort, raised his gun and shot the marshal in the back. Managing to get to his feet, Grat stepped over Connelly's body and started again toward the horses when John Kloehr, one of the marshal's companions, brought him down with a rifle shot. Bill Power fell dead about ten feet farther on but still short of where the horses were tied.[154]

Emmett Dalton was shot in the hip and right arm but managed to mount his horse while still carrying the sack of loot containing more than $20,000 that he and Bob had taken from the First National. He rode back to where Bob had fallen to try to assist his brother onto his horse. As he did so, C.A. Seaman, another member of Connelly's impromptu posse, hit him in the back with a shotgun blast, and Emmett fell beside Bob. Dick Broadwell got on his horse and rode away but not before receiving a load of shot from Seaman's gun and a bullet from Kloehr's rifle. He rode west about a half mile, over the same road he and his outlaw pals had ridden in on, before slumping from the saddle and falling dead to the ground.[155]

Sketch of "Death Alley." Note bodies in upper left portion of sketch. *From the* Coffeyville *Daily Journal.*

Back at Coffeyville, the alley, later dubbed "Death Alley," lay strewn with dead and dying men, and several horses had also been shot. The *Coffeyville Weekly Journal* described the ghastly scene: "Four men lay dead inside of a space of thirty feet long and ten feet wide. Three horses were lying near the men, in the agonies of death, and another one went down a few moments later. Five Winchesters were scattered at different points, and the hard ground and stones were bespattered with human blood."[156]

Emmett Dalton, the only gang member not either dead or breathing his last, readily threw up his uninjured arm and surrendered when ordered to do so. He was taken to a local doctor's office, where his wounds were treated and bandaged. Broadwell's body was brought back to town in a wagon and laid out alongside the bodies of his three dead confederates at the city jail, where an enterprising photographer took pictures of the scene. Hundreds of curious people poured into Coffeyville throughout the afternoon and evening to get a glimpse of the dead bandits and hear eyewitness accounts of the morning's spectacular action.[157]

The city went into mourning for the four townspeople who'd died battling the Dalton Gang, and the businesses remained closed the next couple of days for the men's funerals. Meanwhile, the four dead outlaws were buried without ceremony on Thursday, the day after the shootout.[158]

Bodies of Bob and Grat Dalton propped up for display by local citizens. *Kansas State Historical Society*.

In the aftermath of the gunfight, four area residents said they'd met the outlaws on Wednesday morning west of Coffeyville as they were riding into town to attempt their bold robbery, and all four swore there were six members of the gang at that time. Others swore, however, that there were only five men when the gang reached the edge of town. Who the mysterious "sixth rider" was and what happened to him remains an enigma that is still argued to this day.[159]

Emmett Dalton survived his wounds and reluctantly pled guilty to second-degree murder for the killing of Cubine. He was sentenced to life imprisonment. Pardoned by the Kansas governor after fourteen years, he later cashed in on his Coffeyville notoriety by making movies and writing a book about the infamous raid.[160]

In 1963, the Dalton Defenders Museum opened in Coffeyville to honor the memory of the four citizens who died protecting the town from the Dalton gang: Lucius Baldwin, Charlie Brown, Charles Connelly, and George Cubine. In addition to touring the museum, which contains giant photos of the four defenders and the four dead outlaws among its displays, visitors may explore other points of interest throughout Coffeyville, including the Condon Bank building, "Death Alley," and the graves of the Daltons. Coffeyville also holds an annual Dalton Defenders Days festival each fall.

9

# AS BAD AS THE BENDERS?

## THE NOTORIOUS STAFFLEBACK CLAN

After several members of the Staffleback family were arrested for killing Frank Galbreath in Galena, Kansas, in the summer of 1897 and were suspected of several other murders, newspaper headlines routinely said the Stafflebacks rivaled the Benders or were as "Bad as the Benders." Some even called them "Worse than the Benders." Although the headlines were rather blatant exaggerations, Nancy "Old Lady" Staffleback and her hellish clan did call to mind the notorious family from neighboring Labette County whose backyard gravesite had yielded up the bodies of about ten murder victims twenty-four years earlier.[161]

On the morning of July 19, 1897, a southeast Kansas man named Passwaters was tramping into Galena along Cemetery Road (West Seventh Street). Out of curiosity, he paused about a quarter mile west of Main Street to look into an old abandoned mine shaft that sat just off the road to the north. He was horrified to discover a dead body floating atop the water in the shaft. Word quickly reached Main Street, and soon, a crowd of curious onlookers gathered around the shaft. The body was pulled up and identified as that of Frank Galbreath. Galena city marshal Milford Parker recalled seeing Galbreath drinking in the company of another young man on a Saturday night a few weeks earlier, but nobody had seen him since—until now. Although the body was decomposed, Galbreath had obviously been murdered before being thrown into the shaft. Two bullet wounds were apparent, and the victim's throat had been cut.[162]

A local justice empaneled a jury to view the body, and that evening, Coroner Charles Huffman arrived from Columbus, the Cherokee County seat, to begin an inquest. Galbreath's body was buried the same evening. After deliberating for a couple of days, the coroner's jury adjourned until Monday, July 26, to allow more time to gather evidence.[163]

Suspicion soon settled on the Staffleback family, who lived in a three-room shack on "hell's half acre" just off Seventh Street in the vicinity of the abandoned mine shaft. Besides the Staffleback family, several young women stayed at the place, and it was considered a house of prostitution. In addition to the unsavory reputation of the Stafflebacks and the proximity of their house to the mine shaft, the fact that mysterious gunshots had been heard in the vicinity of their home on or about the night Galbreath disappeared aroused suspicion against them.[164]

The Stafflebacks had lived in the southwest Missouri towns of Joplin and Mount Vernon off and on for about twenty years prior to coming to Galena in early 1896. The father, a candy maker who'd immigrated from Switzerland, was considered a harmless, inoffensive old man. But his wife, Nancy, and the couple's grown sons—Ed, Alonzo, Michael, and George—were considered notorious characters. Alonzo "Johnny" Staffleback was considered a "dangerous lunatic" as early as July 1878, when he went on a spree one night in East Joplin and damaged the property of several neighbors. In the 1880s, the family moved to Mount Vernon, where Nancy filed for divorce from her husband in 1887. She quickly hooked up with Charles Wilson, although it's not clear whether she ever legally married Wilson. In 1889, Nancy and her son Michael got arrested for petit theft, and in 1894, Michael was sent to the Missouri State Penitentiary for larceny. Returning to Joplin, Old Lady Staffleback was arrested as part of a burglary ring in 1895 and later the same year was implicated as a possible accomplice in the killing of an old man named Rosenbaum. In early 1896, Michael got out of prison, and the Staffleback family, minus Alonzo and his father, crossed the state line to Galena.[165]

And now the whole family was in trouble again. Following up on Marshal Parker's recollection that he'd seen Galbreath carousing with another young man on a Saturday night a few weeks earlier, Cherokee County deputy sheriff Charles Rains identified the dead man's drinking partner as Jesse Jacobs and tracked him down in Galena. Jacobs said he had been drinking with Galbreath on the night of June 19 and had accompanied him at about 10:00 p.m. to a "house of ill-fame" run by Nancy Staffleback on the west edge of Galena. Galbreath asked to see Emma Chapman, Nancy's daughter, but he

*Left*: Nancy "Old Lady" Staffleback. *Below*: Sketch of Ed, George, and Mike Staffleback. *From the* St. Louis Republic.

was told Emma was otherwise engaged and to come back later. Returning to Main Street, the men resumed their revel until about 2:00 a.m., when Jacobs announced he was ready to call it a night. As the men parted, Galbreath said he wanted to keep drinking, and he expressed his determination to go back to the Staffleback house. Jacobs said that was the last time he'd seen Galbreath alive.[166]

Since Galbreath's disappearance, George Staffleback had been arrested on a larceny charge, and four other occupants of the Staffleback house—Cora Staffleback, Annie McCombs, Rosa Bayne, and Kirk Carpenter—had vacated the premises. On the evening of July 27, Deputy Rains and several other Kansas officials crossed the state line, located the foursome in a "free and easy" in Joplin, and brought them back to Galena on suspicion of involvement in Galbreath's murder. All four suspects agreed to turn state's evidence, and both Annie and Cora, George's wife, told their stories of the crime almost immediately after they were arrested.[167]

Taking up the narrative where Jesse Jacobs had left off, Annie said Galbreath returned to the Staffleback house about three o'clock in the morning on June 20 and once again asked to see Emma Chapman. Old Lady Staffleback met him at the door and told him Emma didn't want to see him, but Galbreath refused to leave, arguing that Emma had sent him a note asking to see him and that he was determined go in the house and find out for himself whether she wanted to see him. Nancy Staffleback grabbed a corn knife and started after Galbreath, exclaiming, "Let me at him, I'll kill him with this corn knife."[168]

Ed Staffleback and Charles Wilson appeared on the scene wielding pistols and chased Galbreath toward Seventh Street, with Annie and Cora following behind. Ed Staffleback fired at the fleeing man, but Galbreath kept running until a second shot brought him to his hands and knees. When he started to rise, either Staffleback or Wilson stepped up and fired a third shot at him. Still struggling to get up, Galbreath threw up one of his hands, and Ed Staffleback pulled out a pocket knife and slashed him across the face and throat.[169]

Annie rushed up to Ed and tried to pull him away. "Don't, you'll kill him," she cried. Seeing she was too late, she added, "You have killed him now."[170]

Ed threatened to kill Annie, too, if she told anybody what she had witnessed, and he ordered her and Cora back to the house. After the women retreated a short distance, they paused to look back and saw Staffleback and Wilson rifling through the dead man's pockets. Then they saw the two carry the victim to the mine shaft and heard the splash of the water when they dropped him in. When Ed Staffleback came back to the house a short time later, his mother gave him clean clothes to change into. The next morning, Annie saw Charles Wilson cleaning a hat that looked like the one Galbreath had been wearing the night before.[171]

Cora confirmed Annie's story and added that, during the attack on Galbreath, her husband, George, was standing near her. When Annie tried to interfere in the attack, George remarked to Cora, "Why the hell don't Annie leave Ed alone?" Cora also added that George had helped his brother and Charles Wilson dump Galbreath's body in the shaft.[172]

Based on Annie's and Cora's statements, authorities set about the next day rounding up the principal members of the Staffleback gang. George was easily located, since he was already residing in a cell at Columbus awaiting trial on the larceny charge. His brother Mike had been in custody on a similar charge since before Galbreath's disappearance and was, therefore, never accused in the murder. Ed Staffleback was found on the streets of Galena, and his mother was also taken into custody. Charles Wilson was not immediately located. In raiding the Staffleback house, officers found the corn knife with which Nancy had threatened Galbreath and the still-bloody pocketknife with which Ed had slashed the victim's throat.[173]

On July 28, the same day the suspects were rounded up, they appeared before a deputy county attorney in Galena and waived their preliminary hearings. Ed and his brother George, who'd been brought down from Columbus, were charged with murder and taken to the county jail. Their mother, Nancy, whom the *Galena Evening News* called the "perfect picture of an old hag or witch," was also charged as a principal in the murder. She was temporarily held in the Galena City Jail, because there was no good place to keep her in Columbus. The four suspects arrested in Joplin were charged as accomplices but later released on bond.[174]

When the legal proceedings against the Stafflebacks got underway at Columbus on Friday, September 10, Ed's case was severed from his mother and brother's, while George and Nancy immediately went on trial together for murder. Two of the first witnesses to take the stand were Cora Staffleback and Annie McCombs, who repeated much the same story they had previously told.[175]

During the weekend recess, Cora added a sensational twist to the case when she revealed to officers that Frank Galbreath was not the first victim of the Stafflebacks. More than a year prior to the Galbreath murder, Mike and Ed Staffleback had brought home two prostitutes named Lily and Alice and deposited them in the Staffleback house with orders that they belonged to the brothers and were not to take up with other men. One day, Mike came home and found his girl sitting on a stranger's knee. Mike ordered her off the man's lap, and when she refused, he grabbed her up and slapped her. The other man took off, and Mike hit the young woman across the face. She started fighting back, and the other girl came to her aid. At this point, Ed entered the room and ordered the second girl to stay out of the fight. But when Mike whipped out his pistol and started beating the first girl with it, her friend again came to her aid. Ed then began striking and choking the second girl for interfering, and neither man stopped until both girls were dead. The men temporarily hid the bodies in the house and later that night took them to a nearby mine shaft and dropped them in.[176]

Cora's testimony caused a sensation, and she was taken to Galena to point out the shaft that she thought contained the girls' bodies. Workers spent the next several days taking water from the shaft, first by hand and then by pump. Several hundred curious onlookers gathered around in anticipation, and an opportunistic entrepreneur opened up a lemonade stand.[177]

When the trial resumed the next week, George Staffleback took the stand in his own defense. He broke down and confessed his role in dumping the body but insisted that he was primarily a bystander, that his brother did most of the bloody work, and that his mother was not even present at the scene. Nevertheless, the jury came back on Tuesday, September 14, with a verdict convicting him of first-degree murder and his mother of second-degree murder. A separate jury had already been selected for Ed's case, and his trial got underway while the first jury was still deliberating. Later the same day, Ed was also found guilty of first-degree murder.[178]

As work taking water from the mine shaft at Galena continued, much talk began to circulate about lynching the Stafflebacks if additional bodies were found, and newspaper reporters from across the Midwest and even from New York descended on Cherokee County. Many local people, though, began to doubt Cora's story, and the cries for vigilante justice subsided as day after day passed with the discovery of no additional bodies. The overall sensation surrounding the case began to fade as well, except for the newspaper reporters still infesting Galena and Columbus. The *Galena Evening Times* noted that the case continued to receive much more nationwide notoriety than it deserved, since only one murder could be positively attributed to the Staffleback gang.[179]

A few days after the verdicts were announced, a St. Louis reporter interviewed Old Lady Staffleback at the county jail and induced her to pose for a picture. Nancy told the newsman that she was a Christian and a former Sunday school teacher and that, if her boys had turned out bad, it was against her teaching. The reporter also visited her three sons and concluded that all of them were notorious characters but that Mike, "cold-blooded and heartless," was the only nervy one of the bunch.[180]

On the night of September 20, somebody set the abandoned Staffleback house at the edge of Galena on fire. Attracted by the blaze, other citizens

Staffleback shack shortly before it was burned to the ground by local citizens. *From the* St. Louis Republic.

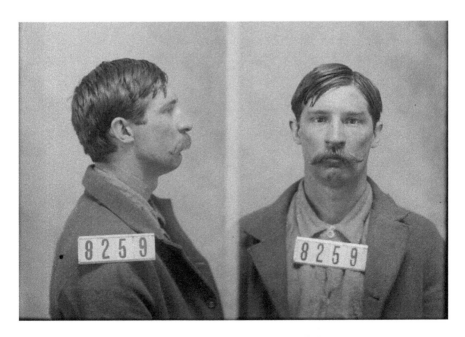

Prison mug shot of George Staffleback. *Kansas State Historical Society.*

arrived, but instead of trying to extinguish it, they stood back and rejoiced as they watched the place burn.[181]

Shortly after his conviction, Ed Staffleback started having "crazy tantrums," and a panel of doctors appointed by the court to investigate his state of mind offered their opinion that he was insane. Acting on the panel's finding, the court undertook an official hearing into Ed's sanity.[182]

On October 1, Judge Andrew Skidmore sentenced Nancy Staffleback to twenty-one years in the Kansas State Penitentiary at Lansing. Skidmore sentenced George to serve one year in the penitentiary and then to be hanged at the end of his one-year term. Mike Staffleback was sentenced to six years in prison for larceny.[183]

Later the same day, Ed Staffleback's insanity claim was denied, and the next day, October 2, he, like his brother, was sentenced to a year in prison followed by hanging. (Both death sentences were later commuted to life imprisonment.) Later the same day, all four Stafflebacks, along with several other convicts, were transported to Lansing.[184]

Charles Wilson was located in late March 1898 at Billings, Missouri, where he had remarried and was living under the name Billy Williams. He admitted he'd lived in Galena with the Stafflebacks at the time Galbreath disappeared, but he insisted that Billy Williams was his real name and that he had not been present at the Staffleback house the night Galbreath was killed. Wilson was nonetheless convicted of second-degree murder after being brought back to Kansas for trial in mid-April, and he joined the Staffleback gang at the Lansing penitentiary.[185]

Ed Staffleback died in prison in 1899. Mike was released in 1902, went on to other misadventures, and wound up back in his old home at the Missouri State Penitentiary. Nancy "Old Lady" Staffleback died in prison at Lansing in 1909. At the time, her son George and her ex-husband, Charles Wilson, were still serving their terms. Cora Staffleback was granted a divorce soon after George was sent to prison, and she remarried in October 1898.[186]

A number of years ago, an old two-story house on Main Street in Galena purporting to be the old Staffleback home opened for tours. Styling itself the "Galena Bordello," the place was fairly successful for a while. In fact, the real Staffleback bordello, which was little more than a shack, burned to the ground more than 120 years ago. The Galena City Hall complex now sits in the general vicinity where the infamous Staffleback den once stood.

# THE KILLING OF CLARA CASTLE AND THE MURDER TRIAL OF JESSIE MORRISON

## ONE OF THE MOST FAMOUS CRIMINAL CASES EVER

O n the morning of June 22, 1900, less than two weeks after Clara Wiley married Guy Olin Castle, Jessie Morrison, with whom Castle had previously kept company, slashed the newly wedded wife to death with a razor in the Castles' El Dorado, Kansas home. On this much, both the defense and prosecution agreed during Jessie's subsequent first-degree murder trial, but who provoked the deadly encounter and exactly how it unfolded were matters of contentious debate. Did Jessie act in self-defense, as she claimed, or did she murder her rival in a jealous rage, as the state charged?[187]

The twenty-nine-year-old Morrison had first met Castle in August 1897 when he came to work at the Racket Store in El Dorado, where she was also employed. Jessie and Olin, who was seven years her junior, went out together occasionally until he met and started courting twenty-six-year-old Clara Wiley about a year later. But even then, he didn't stop seeing Jessie altogether. He became engaged to Clara in October 1898, but he didn't tell Jessie until several months later. Even after Jessie quit the store about January 1900 and went to Excelsior Springs, Missouri, to visit a sister, she and Olin exchanged letters and continued to have "friendly relations." Not until March 1900, shortly before Jessie returned to El Dorado, did he begin trying to break off his relationship with her.[188]

But Jessie did not take well to rejection, at least according to Olin's later testimony. She made periodic trips to the store to see him after she returned from Excelsior Springs. She wanted him to meet her outside of work, threatening him on one occasion that he would regret it if he didn't. Late on the evening of June 11, just two days before Olin and Clara were to be married, Jessie accosted him on the street as he was returning home from Clara's house. Jessie wanted him to go with her to the park, but he brushed her aside and continued home. Jessie came back to the Racket Store in the afternoon of June 20, just two days before the deadly encounter at the Castle home, but Olin, now a married man, walked away when she approached his department.[189]

Between 8:30 and 8:45 on Friday morning, June 22, 1900, Emma Spangler, who resided on Merchant Street in El Dorado, next door to Olin and Clara Castle, heard two voices screaming. At first, she thought it was just kids playing, but the screaming continued for two or three minutes. She also heard the sound of glass breaking, and she realized the sounds were coming from the Castle home. She ran next door, looked in through the screen door, and saw a woman lying on the floor bathed in blood. Finding the screen door locked, she hurried to the back door and found it locked as well. Back at the front of the house, she saw Bettie Moberly, who lived across the street, emerge from her house, and Spangler yelled for her to come and help.[190]

Moberly broke the screen and forced an entry into the Castle home. She found Clara Castle on the floor in a pool of blood with her throat sliced to pieces and Jessie Morrison kneeling over her. When Moberly took hold of Jessie's shoulder to pull her away from Clara, Jessie, who was also bleeding freely from several gashes, jumped up and ran out the door, straight into Emma Spangler. Emma took hold of Jessie's arms and demanded to know what had happened. "I have killed Mrs. Castle," Jessie exclaimed. "I cut her throat with a razor, but she tried to kill me."[191]

The victim, Clara Wiley Castle. *From the St. Louis Post-Dispatch.*

The accused murderer, Jessie Morrison. *From the* St. Louis Republic.

Jessie wanted to go back into the Castle home to retrieve a letter she had dropped. She tried momentarily to break from Emma Spangler's grasp but then let the other woman lead her toward the Morrison home a block away. Inside the house, Jessie dropped onto a bed while Spangler summoned Jessie's mother and gave a general alarm.[192]

Emma Spangler then returned to the Castle residence, where Clara lay in critical condition with her windpipe severed and her esophagus partially severed. Although she couldn't speak, she motioned for writing materials and wrote on a piece of paper, "Jessie Morrison killed me."[193]

Doctors who hurried to Clara's aid inserted a tube in her windpipe so that she could breathe. Later the same day, they operated to reattach the windpipe and esophagus and to sew up her other wounds, but they held out little hope for her recovery. They tried at first feeding her through a tube inserted into her stomach, but Clara could not retain the food, retching it through a hole in the esophagus into the windpipe. They finally resorted to giving her nourishment through injections.[194]

Law officers also rushed to the scene to investigate. Clara responded to their questions by writing her answers. She said Jessie Morrison had come to her door and made some remark. Clara invited Jessie inside to talk, and they sat down. Jessie handed her a letter, asking whether Clara had written it. Clara said no. The next thing she knew, Jessie was attacking her with a razor. She tried to resist, but Jessie continued slashing her as the two women struggled. Clara said that, just before Bettie Moberly entered the house, she saw Jessie cut her own throat.[195]

Jessie also received medical attention, but her wounds were not critical. She told a decidedly different story from what Clara said. Jessie claimed Clara had called her to the door as she was passing the Castle home. After the two went inside, Clara latched the screen door, and the two women sat down. Jessie said Clara accused her of trying to come between the newlyweds and, when Jessie denied it, Clara called her a liar. Jessie told Clara not to call her a liar and got up to leave, dropping her handkerchief as she did so. When she stooped to pick it up, Clara retrieved a razor from a nearby dresser and attacked her with it. Jessie fell to the floor, kicked furiously at Clara, and finally succeeded in wresting the razor away from her. She then slashed Clara with the razor, but only because she feared for her own life.[196]

Investigators recovered a bloody razor, presumed to be the murder weapon, from the scene. They also found the letter that Jessie had wanted to go back into the house to retrieve. It was from Jessie's sister in Excelsior Springs, and it contained no mention of the Castles. Most people, finding no reason to doubt the dying woman's story, speculated that Jessie had asked Clara to read the letter only as a decoy, but Jessie denied that she'd even mentioned the letter to Clara. She said she simply happened to be carrying it when Clara called her to the door.[197]

As Clara grew increasingly weaker, her composure and equanimity in the face of imminent death elicited the sympathy of the entire community. On July 5, she wrote several "good bye" notes to her friends and even wrote "a pathetic note of forgiveness" to Jessie Morrison. Jessie sent a verbal response that she had nothing against Clara and was sorry that she appeared to be dying. In reporting the story, one newspaper praised Clara's demeanor and behavior as "absolutely saintly."[198]

Clara finally succumbed during the early morning of July 10. Jessie was promptly lodged in the Butler County Jail and later moved to an upstairs room of the courthouse, charged with first-degree murder. Clara's funeral, which an El Dorado newspaper called "one of the largest the city has ever known," was held the next day, and she was buried in the local Belle Vista Cemetery.[199]

Jessie's preliminary examination before Justice B.F. Allebach began on July 17. The women who discovered Clara on the floor of her home with Jessie kneeling over her, the doctors who treated Clara, and the law officers who conducted the initial investigation were among the state's witnesses. Olin Castle also took the stand to describe Jessie's seeming obsession with him, and several employees of Racket's Store confirmed that Jessie repeatedly visited the store after she no longer worked there. When the hearing ended on July 20, Justice Allebach ordered that Jessie be held without bond on a charge of first-degree murder.[200]

Jessie's lawyers immediately filed a writ of habeas corpus with probate judge J.M. Randall, saying the evidence against their client was not strong enough to hold her without bail. Randall ordered a hearing on the motion to be held in mid-August. At the new hearing, he sustained the verdict of the original examination and ordered that Jessie be held without bail.[201]

Sketch of Olin Castle, the object of a lethal love triangle, sitting in court. *From the* St. Louis Post-Dispatch.

When Jessie's trial began on November 23, 1900, the state sought to show that the defendant had gone to the Castle home with the intention of killing Clara, that she brought the murder weapon with her, and that she attacked the victim without provocation. Emma Spangler was one of the state's key witnesses. She testified that, when she first looked into the Castle home after hearing the screams, Clara was already covered with blood but that she saw no blood or wounds on Jessie. In keeping with their theory that Jessie had taken the murder weapon with her to the crime scene, prosecutors called several witnesses who testified that Jessie had made repeated trips to the Racket Store in the days leading up to the murder and that she had been seen on more than one occasion near the case in which razors were kept. The defense tried to keep a statement that Clara dictated a few days before her death from being admitted as evidence, but the judge ruled in favor of the prosecution. In her dying statement, Clara said that Jessie asked whether the two women were friends, and Clara said they were not because of Jessie's attempts to come between her and Olin. Jessie then handed Clara the letter to read and attacked her as soon as she took the letter and started reading.[202]

The highlight of the trial occurred on December 7, when Jessie Morrison, who was the daughter of ex–county judge M.H. Morrison, took the stand in her own defense. She said she did not take a razor to the Castle home. She said the reason she had the letter with her was that she had left home to see about a dress she was making and that she thought the letter would make a good paper to cut the collar pattern from. She said that she only went to the Castle home because Clara called her in and that she acted strictly in self-defense when she killed Clara. Jessie said she did not pursue Olin Castle after he became engaged to Clara and did not accost him on the streets of El Dorado at night shortly before his wedding, as he claimed. To the contrary, Olin was the one who was reluctant to break off their relationship. When she mentioned this to Clara, telling her that Olin was the one who was creating friction and trying to make her jealous, Clara called her a liar. When Jessie said not to call her a liar, Clara went into a rage, shoving Jessie and attacking her with a razor after Jessie shoved her back. In their closing arguments, the defense lawyers pointed out the calm composure with which their client had faced the jurors and the prosecuting witnesses throughout her trial, while Olin Castle had avoided looking at Jessie or her lawyers during his testimony.[203]

Jessie's trial ended in a mistrial when the jurors came back on the morning of December 14 and told the judge they were hopelessly deadlocked. The jurors reportedly stood nine for acquittal and three for conviction, which came as a surprise to many observers because they thought general sentiment favored the prosecution. One of the jurors who had voted for acquittal said he and several of the other jurors were impressed by Jessie's testimony and thought that she came across on the stand as very believable. He added that he might have given more credence to Clara's dying statement if she had written it herself.[204]

A new trial, originally set for the March 1901 session of the Butler County District Court, was continued until June and got underway about the middle of the month. The trial made headlines across the country, just as the first one had, and out-of-town reporters flocked to El Dorado to cover the proceedings. The courtroom was packed for many of the sessions, with most of the spectators being women, and all eyes were on the defendant. Everybody wanted to know what Jessie was wearing, what her demeanor was, and how she was holding up under the strain. Typical of the reporting was the *El Dorado Republican*'s observation as court began on June 14: "The morning was very warm and Miss Morrison was attired in a cool white summer dress, wore a yellow and blue silk sash and white sailor hat." The same newspaper later remarked on Jessie's wonderful composure and self-possession, even as incriminating testimony against her was being given.[205]

A key difference between the second trial and the first one was that several statements in Clara's own handwriting, which she had penned during her dying days but which had not been introduced at the first trial, were placed into evidence by the state. They generally agreed with the statement she had dictated to the county attorney, which had been introduced at the first trial, but jurors found the dying statements in Clara's own hand more convincing than one she had merely dictated. Jessie's case suffered another setback when a man named Morgan—whose affidavit swearing that he had heard Clara call Jessie into her house was presented into evidence at the first trial—did not show up to testify, and one of Jessie's lawyers was suspected of having falsified the affidavit. Although Jessie again took the stand in her own defense and told essentially the same story she'd told at the first trial, this time, the jurors found her guilty of manslaughter in the second degree. The verdict, rendered on June 27 after thirty hours of deliberation, was a compromise, because the first vote stood eleven to one in favor of a first-degree murder conviction. The one holdout refused to vote even for a second-degree murder conviction; so, the rest of the jurors agreed to the lesser charge in order to get any conviction at all.[206]

A defense motion for a new trial was denied, and Judge Granville Aikman, who was among the many who felt Jessie had gotten off too easily, sentenced her to five years in the state penitentiary, the maximum allowed for second-degree manslaughter. She was escorted to the state prison at Lansing on July 9, and all along the way, people turned out to get a glimpse of the celebrated prisoner.[207]

Still not giving up, Jessie's lawyers appealed to the Kansas Supreme Court, and Jessie was released on bond in early September, pending the hearing. At its January 1902 term, the high court ruled that a number of prospective jurors should have been disqualified because they admitted during jury selection that they already entertained an opinion as to the defendant's guilt. The supreme court overturned the verdict of the lower court and remanded the case to Butler County for a new trial.[208]

As it turned out, Jessie and her lawyers should have been satisfied that she got off as easily as she did with only a five-year sentence. At her third trial, in June 1902, the courtroom was "packed like sardines in a box" as Jessie again testified in her own defense, but once again, the jurors gave more credence to Clara's dying declarations than they did to Jessie's story of the crime. The defendant was convicted of second-degree murder, and Judge Aikman sentenced her to twenty-five years in prison. He overruled a motion for a new trial, and she was transported back to Lansing on Sunday evening, July 13.[209]

Jessie's lawyers again appealed her case to the Kansas Supreme Court, and she was released on bond in early October pending the outcome of the hearing. In May 1903, however, the high court affirmed the lower court's verdict. Jessie cried when informed of the decision, maintaining still that she had acted only in self-defense. The Kansas Supreme Court denied a petition for a rehearing of the case, and Jessie was transported on June 10 back to the state penitentiary, where she worked as a seamstress.[210]

Efforts to win Jessie's freedom continued almost unabated for several years after she returned to prison, and she was finally paroled in late September 1910 by Governor W.R. Stubbs after serving seven years of her twenty-five-year term. In announcing his decision, Stubbs reportedly said that he felt Jessie's first trial, at which nine men voted for acquittal and three for conviction, was probably the fairest one she had received and that he thought twenty-five years in prison was excessive. Upon her release, Jessie traveled first to her sister's home in Excelsior Springs, where she was briefly interviewed. She said she was happy to be free, not just for herself but also for her aged and ailing father, who had spent his life on her behalf. The reporter remarked, however, that even in Jessie's "gayest moments" one could detect a "prison pallor," which had left its stamp on her features, and that she showed every bit of her thirty-eight years.[211]

Jessie took a job as a saleslady in an Excelsior Springs dry-goods store, and she later went to stay with her father at El Reno, Oklahoma, where he had moved. In February 1913, Governor George Hodges pardoned Jessie, granting her unconditional freedom. It was noted at the time that Jessie had been a model prisoner and that she had maintained a spotless record after her parole. About the time the pardon was announced, Jessie returned to her native West Virginia to live with relatives. Olin Castle had long ago left Kansas as well, having moved to California and remarried in 1903.[212]

Because of the sensational nature of the crime and because the defendant, the victim, and the victim's husband all came from prominent families, the Jessie Morrison case not only captivated local residents, who knew the principals, but also attracted attention throughout the state and the nation. In 1913, about the time of Jessie's pardon, the *El Dorado Walnut Valley Times* recalled that the case had "excited more interest than any other tragedy in the history of Butler County—or possibly Kansas," and in October 1923, more than twenty-three years after Clara Castle's death, the rival *El Dorado Republican* remembered the case as "one of the most famous criminal cases ever tried in the country."[213]

# 11

# I'LL NOT LET ANY MAN ABUSE MY SISTER

## A CASE OF JUSTIFIABLE HOMICIDE

O n Thursday morning, June 23, 1904, twenty-seven-year-old George Pritchett learned that his brother-in-law, Ed Bockemuehl, had been carrying on with a woman who lived upstairs from the Bockemuehls in rooms over 215 Main Street in Wichita. It was just the latest example of Ed's heartless treatment of his wife, May. George, who lived across the hall from the couple, had seen his older sister suffer enough. He meant to put a stop to it.[214]

Later that morning, he called at the Manhattan Hotel, where Ed worked as a bartender, and told his brother-in-law he had to quit seeing other women and otherwise mistreating May. The forty-one-year-old Bockemuehl did not take well to the reprimand. He told George to tend to his own business or he would "fix him."[215]

As it turned out, Ed Bockemuehl should have paid more attention to George's warning.

Originally from Illinois, Bockemuehl had been previously married to a woman named Bessie, with whom he had two children, but he deserted his wife and kids about 1899 and went to live with the Marian Pritchett family in Peoria as a boarder. Bockemuehl struck up a romance with Marian's daughter May, and when Bessie and her kids came to visit, he at first told May that Bessie was his sister. May quickly learned the truth, though, and she demanded that Bockemuehl legally separate from his wife before she would have anything more to do with him. Bockemuehl obtained a divorce from Bessie in February 1902 and married May seven months later. Shortly afterward, the couple moved to Wichita. George followed his sister to Kansas, married a Wichita woman named Maude Osborne, and took up residence in the same boardinghouse where his sister and Bockemuehl lived.[216]

Bockemuehl, who'd been a bartender most of his adult life, usually got along fairly well with his customers, and he had a host of friends. However, he was quick to anger, and, out of sight of the public eye, he was especially abusive toward his wife. He'd mistreated her almost from the time he and May married, but the abuse had gotten worse in recent weeks.[217]

One afternoon in mid-June, May went to the Manhattan bar and found Ed flirting with two women. May ordered them to leave, but Ed said they didn't have to and that his wife was the one who must leave. Ed put May out, but she came back and once again confronted the two women. "You get out of here and go home," Ed told May, "or I will shoot you." May left feeling humiliated, and when the quarrel resumed that night after Ed got home, he verbally abused her, struck her, and choked her.[218]

In spite of Ed's brutish behavior, May, who was a "good-looking, pleasant-appearing woman" about thirty years old, loved her husband, and she didn't say a word to anyone about the mistreatment she received at his hands, not even to her brother.[219]

She didn't say a word until she ran into Jennie Colburn, on old friend from Peoria who was in Wichita as a singer in a traveling vaudeville show. Recognizing Jennie on the streets shortly after the choking incident, May greeted her with surprise, then threw her arms around Jennie's neck and started crying. "Oh, Jennie," she confessed, "I married Ed, who I went with so long in Peoria, and he is now going with other women and I can hardly stand it. You don't know what a life I am leading." May told her friend in confidence about the mistreatment she habitually suffered at Ed's hands.[220]

A woman named Blanche, who lived one floor up from the Bockemuehls and the Pritchetts in the YMCA building in downtown Wichita, was Ed's latest flirtation. Suspecting that her husband planned to meet Blanche on Tuesday, June 21, May followed Ed that afternoon and caught him and Blanche just as they were getting on a streetcar together. Seeing his wife, Ed got off and walked on up the street, but that night when he got home, he flew into a rage, threatening to kill May. He took out a revolver and pointed it at her head, and May got down on her knees and begged for her life.[221]

Jennie Colburn spent the next night, June 22, at the Bockemuehl residence, and early the next morning, May once again confided in her friend, telling her about Ed's latest cruelty. When Jennie saw George soon afterward, she hinted to him that Ed had been mistreating May. George confronted his sister, and she admitted Ed's flirtation with Blanche but wouldn't tell her brother the full details of her abuse.[222]

George heard enough, though, to harden his resolve against Ed Bockemuehl.

May's revelation that Ed had been carrying on with the woman upstairs wasn't complete news to George. He'd seen Ed and Blanche on the street together, and he'd even seen Ed giving her money recently. Based on what Jennie had said, he could fill in the rest of the blanks for himself without May spelling them out. No man, he decided, was going to keep treating his sister the way Ed had been treating May and get away with it.[223]

But first, he meant to have a talk with Blanche. After Ed left for work on Thursday morning, June 23, George went upstairs to confront her. When he told her to stay away from Ed, she at first denied that she'd been seeing him, but George said he'd seen them on the streets together with his own eyes. Blanche grew defiant and said she would go with whomever she pleased, and George left in anger.[224]

George's clash with Ed at the Manhattan Hotel later the same morning didn't go any better than his set-to with Blanche, and he was still upset when Ed came home for lunch shortly after noon.

But so was Ed.

George came over to the Bockemuehl apartment and sat down in the front room with May and Ed. "Now, Ed," George began, "I am going to talk to you straight and as a gentleman. You must either treat May better or leave her, or else she must leave you. You are killing her by inches, and I can't stand to see it. You need not say you are not doing these things, for I know you are, and you must stop."[225]

Ed jumped up and said, "I'll not allow anybody to dictate to me what to do, and I'll just leave the damned bitch."

George and May followed Ed into the bedroom, where May threw her arms around her husband, begging him piteously to stay. Ed struck his wife, shoved her down into a corner, and kicked her.

"I'll not let any man abuse my sister before my eyes," George said.

"Damn you," Ed retorted. "I'll fix you." He stomped into the kitchen and picked up a butcher knife. George retrieved a pistol from a table in the bedroom, the same pistol with which Ed had threatened May a couple of nights earlier, and he trailed Ed into the kitchen.

Jennie Colburn, who'd been listening to the argument from the kitchen, ran out of the room when the men entered. A shot rang out as she started, and she turned to glimpse Ed clutching his chest. She heard at least two more shots as

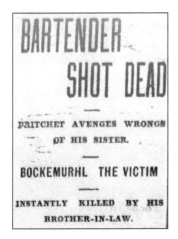

**BARTENDER SHOT DEAD**

PRITCHET AVENGES WRONGS OF HIS SISTER.

BOCKEMURHL THE VICTIM

INSTANTLY KILLED BY HIS BROTHER-IN-LAW.

Newspaper headline tells the story of Ed Bockemuehl's killing. *From the* Wichita Beacon.

she hurried away. May agreed that her brother fired three shots, but neither woman was an eyewitness to the entire encounter.[226]

Two officers arrived quickly after the shooting and found Bockemuehl beyond help. George, who knew one of the lawmen, told them that he would go directly to the police station and turn himself in, and they let him leave. However, he did not show up at the station promptly and was arrested a couple of hours later at another location in Wichita. He still had the revolver in his possession, but officers could not tell how many shots had been fired, as the weapon had been reloaded. George broke down and cried, saying he could not stand to see Ed abuse his sister, but he refused to relate the exact circumstances of the shooting.[227]

Bockemuehl was dead by the time medical help arrived at his and May's apartment. His body was taken to an undertaking establishment, where the county coroner began an examination later the same day. The coroner took one bullet from the dead man's body, and two others were retrieved from the kitchen floor in the Bockemuehl rooms, which seemed to confirm what the women said about the number of shots fired.[228]

An official coroner's inquest was held the next day, June 24. In what came as a surprise to many observers—who thought the evidence favored a verdict of justifiable homicide—the coroner's jury concluded only that "Edward Bockemuehl came to his death by gunshot wounds from a revolver in the hands and used by George Pritchett."[229]

George was arraigned the following day on a charge of murder but released on $4,000 bond. Bockemuehl's funeral was also held on June 25, and his body was afterward shipped back to Illinois for burial, with May accompanying her deceased husband.[230]

In early July, Bessie Bockemuehl filed a claim for part of Ed Bockemuehl's estate, saying Ed had deserted her and her kids and had never gotten a divorce. A week or two later, however, May produced evidence that Ed had indeed obtained a divorce from Bessie, and May was declared Ed's sole heir.[231]

George Prtichett's preliminary hearing began on July 19 in Wichita City Court. Much testimony centered on whether the dead man was shot in the back or in the chest, but the evidence was not clear-cut on the question.

May Bockemuehl took the stand and admitted that her deceased husband was prone to angry demonstrations. She added that he was violent not only toward her but toward other people as well. He had once cut a man with a knife in Illinois; had cut a man in Guthrie, Oklahoma; and had threatened to kill two different Wichita men. Other witnesses, including the defendant's wife, Maude Pritchett, confirmed that Ed was given to violent outbursts and that he often treated his wife cruelly.[232]

At the conclusion of the hearing, the judge declared that George Pritchett had acted in defense of his own life and that of his sister. The case was, therefore, justifiable homicide, and the charges against the defendant were dropped. Once again a free man, George, his wife, and his sister walked out of the courtroom together.[233]

## Chapter 12
# MURDER OR SUICIDE?

## THE MYSTERIOUS DEATH OF MISS MAY SAPP

A fter Caroline May Sapp was found dead with her throat slashed from ear to ear outside her home in Moran, Kansas, on the evening of September 27, 1907, many people thought she'd been the victim of a heinous murder. But from the very beginning there were also those who speculated she might have cut her own throat. Some of those who held to the murder theory pointed to a scandal May had been involved in more than ten years earlier, when she was a seventeen-year-old schoolgirl, as a possible motive for the crime. But most people dismissed such conjecture as farfetched.[234]

As it turned out, those who recalled the decade-old scandal were on the right track.

The daughter of prominent farmer John Sapp, May grew up in the Moran vicinity of eastern Allen County. During the winter of 1896–97, she was enrolled in the rural Walnut Grove school near her home under schoolmaster Samuel F. Whitlow. A sensation developed when a woman allowed her sick little granddaughter to go to school on the condition that she stay inside at recess, but the girl came home from school and reported that Whitlow wouldn't let her stay in because he stayed in himself with May Sapp and locked all the other kids outside during recess. When the little girl's father initiated an investigation, Whitlow denied any wrongdoing. The county superintendent let the schoolmaster off with a stern warning and hushed up the scandal for the good of the school and Miss Sapp's reputation.[235]

A couple of months later, in mid-March 1897, May received a letter, purportedly from a schoolmate named Will Merrifield, asking her to meet him secretly at a hotel in nearby Bronson on the evening of March 17 on an urgent matter. Irate upon seeing the letter, John Sapp demanded an official inquiry. Merrifield quickly proved he did not write the letter, but another young man, Bert Peckham, was arrested and charged with sending indecent mail, because he matched the description of the person who'd come to the post office to see whether May sent a reply. Peckham also denied writing the letter, and the charges against him were eventually dropped. It was whispered among the few people who knew about the school scandal that Sam Whitlow might have been the person who actually wrote the letter, but he was never officially investigated as a suspect.[236]

About 1905, John Sapp retired, and the family moved from their farm east of Moran into town, where Whitlow, having quit teaching, now ran a feed and flour store. As far as the townspeople were concerned, though, Whitlow was a happily married man, and he and May Sapp had no association other than to exchange casual greetings when they occasionally met on the streets. Sapp was twenty-six years old, still single, and "very attractive in appearance," but no one thought it particularly odd that she rarely went out with young men. She had a host of friends and was considered a "most estimable" young lady.[237]

About 7:25 p.m. on Friday evening, September 27, 1907, May and her mother, Rebecca Sapp, were sitting in their home in Moran engaged in casual conversation when May rose from her chair and stepped outside onto the back porch. Just moments later, Rebecca heard her daughter's piercing cry, "Mother! Mother!"[238]

Miss Caroline May Sapp, the Murdered Girl.

When May Sapp was found dead with her throat slashed, many assumed she was murdered, as the caption for this image indicates. *From the* Topeka State Journal.

Rebecca Sapp jumped up and ran outside in answer to the scream. She found May lying in the yard near a poultry pen a short distance from the porch with a ghastly cut across her throat and blood gushing out. Horrified, Rebecca started screaming, and two passersby rushed to the scene. Soon, the whole neighborhood was aroused, but May Sapp was beyond help.[239]

John Sapp, who'd walked downtown just a few minutes earlier, hurried back home when he heard someone say his daughter was dead. Convinced that May had been murdered, he joined in scouring the crime scene for clues and searching for his daughter's assailant. Several neighbors told of having seen a mysterious man in the alley at the rear of the Sapp home, but no solid leads were developed.[240]

Coroner David Reid, County Attorney Carl Peterson, and Sheriff Charles Bollinger were summoned from Iola, and they arrived later that night to begin an official inquiry into May's death. Bloodhounds were brought in, but by the time they arrived, the Sapp backyard had been trampled on so much that the dogs proved virtually useless.[241]

Some of the investigating officers thought May might have taken her own life, but her family and friends felt strongly that she had been foully murdered. May, they said, was happy and cheerful and had never seemed morose or melancholy. She was dressed for a party and was getting ready to leave to attend the event when she stepped outside to her death.[242]

Other circumstances pointed to murder as well. The razor that was presumed to be the instrument of death was found about fifteen feet from where May had fallen. Mysteriously, however, it showed virtually no sign of blood, and it was not discovered until late that night, after the body had been removed and taken inside the home. The backyard had been thoroughly and repeatedly gone over by searchers carrying lanterns earlier in the evening, and Mr. Sapp said he would stake his life that the razor was not where it was later found when the grounds were previously searched. Sapp also added that none of his razors were missing from the house. In addition, May's hair and clothing were disheveled, and she had a couple of cuts on one of her hands, as though she might have struggled briefly with an assailant. Family members pointed out, too, that May never referred to Rebecca Sapp as "Mother" but instead routinely called her "Ma." They therefore thought it very likely that May had screamed "Murder!" rather than "Mother!" and that Rebecca had simply misunderstood her daughter's cry. Finally, the severity and depth of the wounds argued against suicide.[243]

"From the very first," noted the *Iola Register* the day after May was found dead, "the case appeared mysterious. Was it suicide or murder?"[244]

One of the investigating officers added: "It is the strangest thing I have ever met with. There is something behind the death that we haven't reached."[245]

The inquest that began on Friday night continued the next day, but when little solid evidence turned up to shed additional light on May's tragic death, the coroner suspended the inquiry until October 7, allowing time to gather more information. After the county officials returned to Iola, the prosecutor received a tip that May might have been pregnant, and the officials hurried back to Moran on Sunday to conduct an autopsy, briefly delaying the funeral service scheduled that day. Held with the help of a local doctor, the autopsy determined that May, in the words of the *Iola Register*, "had no cause to take her life as far as hiding anything that might reflect on her character."[246]

Although May had reportedly soured on religion in recent years, her funeral service, held at the Presbyterian church across the street from her home later on Sunday, was the largest ever held in southeast Kansas. "The church could not hold a fourth of those in attendance," said the *Register*. Burial in the Moran Cemetery followed the service.[247]

By Monday, September 30, local officials and other observers were increasingly convinced that they were looking at a murder, but they were no closer to solving the puzzle than they had been two days earlier. A Pinkerton detective summoned by local authorities arrived that evening and began his investigation the next day. Among the angles the detective began pursuing was a possible link between May's death and the almost-forgotten scandal involving her schoolmaster more than ten years earlier. Local officials gave no credence to this theory. The idea that May might have been killed by a woman was also proffered for the first time.[248]

On Monday, October 7, the inquest into May's death, which was scheduled to resume that day, was postponed when Sam Whitlow told the Pinkerton detective he had important information. The two men went to Whitlow's office, where Whitlow made an incredible confession: he knew May Sapp's death to be a suicide because he had witnessed it.[249]

Whitlow said May had been infatuated with him for more than two years. In August 1905, shortly after the Sapp family moved into Moran, Whitlow was passing the Sapp residence when May hailed him and implored him to come see her later that evening, which he finally consented to do. When he returned, May declared her love for him, saying she could not live without him. She beseeched him to leave his wife and kids, but Whitlow told her he loved his family. Whitlow claimed he did nothing to encourage or reciprocate May's feelings but that she continued to press her suit at every clandestine opportunity. Gradually, her love for him began to manifest itself as anger that he would not leave his wife, rather than as tenderness. In recent weeks, she had started coming to his house at night and calling him out by tapping on a window. She did so again on the Tuesday night before her death. He went out to talk to her, urging her to go back home and give up her infatuation. They remained in the yard contending with each other until the wee hours of the morning. At one point, when Whitlow repulsed

Sketch of accused killer Sam Whitlow as he wrote out his statement. *From the* St. Louis Post-Dispatch.

May's advances, she drew a razor from the folds of her dress and threatened to kill herself, drawing the blade lightly across her throat and also cutting Whitlow's hand. Near 3:00 a.m., Whitlow, by entreaties, finally convinced her to go back home.[250]

The next night, Whitlow went to the Sapp residence and called May out by a prearranged whistle the two used as a signal. Whitlow was afraid that, if he didn't go to her house, she would come back to his. He wanted to convince her once and for all to forgo her pursuit of him, and he also wanted to try to prevent her from carrying through with her threat of self-destruction. The same scene was repeated the next night, Thursday. When Sam came back once again on Friday evening, he announced that he had told his wife about May's obsession with him, and he repeated his determination not to leave his family. He told May they must stop seeing each other. "If that is so," she declared, "I will kill myself as I said I would." She immediately drew the razor and slashed herself twice across the throat, crying out once before cutting herself and once as soon as she inflicted the fatal wounds. Stunned, Whitlow reached for May to try to support her as she collapsed, and he grabbed hold of the razor. Seeing her fall dead or dying at his feet, he raced out of the yard and back to his own home five blocks away, still carrying the bloody razor. He washed the razor, later took it back to the Sapp home, and, when no one was looking, dropped it near the place where May had collapsed. Whitlow said he was prompted to come forward because a confession he'd written out soon after May's death was missing from his home, and he thought that officers had probably already gotten their hands on it.[251]

Monday evening, the prosecutor and other county officers arrived in Moran, and Whitlow repeated his story to them. He denied he'd had an inappropriate relationship with May when he was her teacher, and he said he'd seen her only a very few times since then until the Sapp family moved into Moran. After the questioning, Whitlow was arrested on suspicion and escorted to Iola. During the trip, he consumed some wood alcohol in an apparent suicide attempt, but he revived after Coroner Reid pumped his stomach as soon as the party reached Iola.[252]

A new coroner's jury was empaneled, because one of the members of the previous jury was a relative of Whitlow's. The suspect once again repeated his sensational story to the new jury at the coroner's office in Iola on Tuesday, October 8, and afterward he was cross-examined by the jurors and county officials. Although he admitted that May was good-looking, he maintained that he was not attracted to her and had never touched her except to shake hands with her. He was then grilled as to why, if May Sapp held no attractiveness to him, he continued secretly meeting her time after time over a period of two years. He replied that he was trying to prevent her from doing something rash. He added that he had finally decided the only solution was for him and his family to leave Moran and that he was making preparations to do so when May killed herself. Asked why he did not make his confession immediately after her death, he said that he did not want to bring disgrace to the Sapp family or his and that he decided it might be best to let the incident remain a mystery. He also denied having attempted suicide the previous day, saying instead that he'd thought he was taking grain alcohol mixed with medicine as a remedy for sciatic pain.[253]

Although many people were impressed by Whitlow's unwavering consistency in telling his story, others were not convinced, particularly friends and family of the dead woman. After the inquest was moved to Moran later on Tuesday, the Sapp family doctor, who had examined May immediately after her death, testified that her wounds were more consistent with murder than suicide. Both John and Rebecca Sapp said that they were light sleepers and that they would have known if May had been slipping out of the house late at night as often as Whitlow claimed. Mrs. Sapp added that not enough time had elapsed after her daughter left the house on the fateful night before she heard her cry out for May's death to have been preceded by an argument, as Whitlow said.[254]

The next day, Wednesday, the inquest resumed with thirty-three-year-old May Whitlow, Sam's wife, as the star witness. She corroborated parts of Sam's story, such as the fact that he had told her on the afternoon before May Sapp's death about the young woman's infatuation with him. When a juror suggested that this knowledge might have made her jealous and that she herself might have had something to do with May's death, she strongly denied the allegation. She did admit, though, that she at first doubted Sam's statement to her that he had never been intimate with Miss Sapp.[255]

Sam Whitlow was grilled by the jury again on Thursday, but he did not waver under the insistent questioning. If his story was untrue, observed the *Iola Register*, "he is certainly a remarkably smooth man."[256]

Few people believed that Whitlow had never been intimate with May Sapp, but many believed the major points of his story, including the immediate circumstances surrounding May's death. Others were thoroughly convinced that May had been murdered. The coroner's jury only added to the division and confusion when it concluded late Thursday that May Sapp had been killed by someone other than herself, but that this person was unknown to the jury.[257]

Nevertheless, Whitlow was officially charged with murder the next morning, Friday, October 11, on a complaint filed by May's father, John Sapp. Despite the ambiguous verdict of the coroner's jury, Prosecutor Peterson felt the facts warranted such a charge.[258]

Interviewed in mid-October, Bert Peckham, the man who'd been officially accused in the decade-old scandal, said that Whitlow might not have been the person who came to the Bronson post office seeking a reply to the letter

May Sapp had received, but that he (Peckham) knew Whitlow had called at the Bronson hotel in anticipation of meeting May there clandestinely. Peckham allowed that Whitlow might have been trying to sever ties with May in the days or weeks before her death, but he thought it was nonsense to believe that Whitlow had never returned May's affection in any way.[259]

Whitlow's preliminary hearing began at Moran on October 24 before Justice C.S. Potter. Coroner Reid offered his opinion that May Sapp's wounds could not have been self-inflicted, but little additional new evidence was presented. When the hearing ended the next day, Potter ordered Whitlow held for trial on a $10,000 bond. He was taken back to jail at Iola but was released on bond a few days later. After his release, he returned to Moran, where he had a brief confrontation with John Sapp on the street three days later. Shortly after that, Whitlow closed his business in Moran and moved to Iola.[260]

First scheduled for the January 1908 term of the Allen County District Court, Whitlow's trial was continued until May. The proceedings got underway on May 19, and the courtroom at Iola was "jammed to the utmost" for almost every session.[261]

Bent not only on proving Whitlow guilty of murder but also on vindicating May Sapp's honor, the prosecution portrayed Sapp as an ideal young lady who was refined and cheerful with absolutely no reason to kill herself. The state's attorneys rejected the whole idea that Whitlow and Sapp had been carrying on a two-year clandestine relationship. They ridiculed Whitlow's confession as a lie he'd fabricated shortly after May's death and rehearsed for several days before coming forward. It was incredible to think, they said, that he had met May secretly more than one hundred times, as he claimed, without May Whitlow or anyone else finding out about the affair. Instead, said the prosecution, Whitlow was a lustful cretin who had been obsessed with May Sapp ever since he'd fallen for her when she was his seventeen-year-old student, and he'd finally acted on his desperate yearning on the night of September 27, 1907. She had defended herself as he tried to force himself on her, and he killed her to keep her from reporting the attack. The circumstances of May's death and most of the expert testimony suggested murder, the state concluded, while the only evidence of suicide was the defendant's own statement.[262]

The defense, on the other hand, sought to show that May Sapp was insanely infatuated with Whitlow and had indeed been meeting him secretly for two years, just as Whitlow said. The reason she rarely, if ever, kept company with young men, the defense lawyers argued, was because she was in love with Whitlow, a married man. They put witnesses on the stand who'd heard May state or hint as much. They also produced witnesses who'd seen a young man and a young woman together near the Sapp or Whitlow residence at various times after dark fitting the description of May and the defendant. May Whitlow, who slept in a separate room from her husband, testified that she had heard unusual noises outside her home at nighttime in recent weeks. Both she and her young son stated that on various occasions they had found things mysteriously rearranged or broken at their home, just as Whitlow said May had done. May Whitlow also confirmed various other parts of her husband's story, and the defense even produced a lock of hair that May Sapp had allegedly cut from her own head and wrapped around a doorknob at the Whitlow home late one night. Whitlow's lawyers admitted that his story was a remarkable one, but its marvelous aspect, they said, did not make it untrue.[263]

The jurors apparently agreed. On May 31, after deliberating for thirty-six hours, they came back with a not guilty verdict. A report leaked that the jury was initially split nine to three for acquittal but that the three holdouts for conviction gradually came around.[264]

Almost from the time Sam Whitlow came forward with his sensational story, few people believed there had not been some sort of secret relationship between him and May Sapp. If the prosecution had accepted the affair and developed a motive for the crime other than Whitlow's animal lusts, the outcome of the trial might have been different. Had the state suggested, for instance, that the crime happened during an argument as Whitlow attempted to break off the affair, a verdict of second-degree murder might well have resulted. By their insistence on upholding May's virtue, prosecutors likely forfeited their best hope of convicting the man who was, at least indirectly, responsible for her death.

Angry and shaken by the verdict, John Sapp insisted on pursuing the case against Whitlow. In July, Whitlow was arrested for perjury on a complaint from Sapp, alleging that Whitlow had lied at the first coroner's jury in saying he knew nothing about May Sapp's death and again at trial in saying that she had killed herself. Sapp was again disappointed, however, when Whitlow was acquitted on all counts of the perjury charge in September.[265]

# THE MURDER OF ELLA SCOTT

## THE MOST SENSATIONAL CASE LINN COUNTY EVER HAD

A fter thirty-two-year-old Eleanor "Ella" Scott was killed under mysterious circumstances at her home in La Cygne, Kansas, in mid-June 1923, a few people began to whisper that her husband, J. Ellison Scott, might have murdered her. But the large majority of folks in La Cygne and throughout Linn County brushed aside the rumors. Even after the county prosecutor announced that he was bringing charges of murder against Ellison Scott, most people stood by the thirty-one-year-old, a man many had known all his life. Everything changed in an instant, though, when evidence was brought out that Scott had been secretly carrying on with his wife's nineteen-year-old niece, Arlene.[266]

Both John Ellison Scott and Ella Holt had grown up in Linn County, and their families were well known throughout the county. The couple married at Centerville in 1911. They then lived a few years at Cadmus before moving to La Cygne, where Ellison opened a grocery and meat market. In the fall of 1919, Arlene Scott, Ella's teenage niece, came to stay with the childless couple in La Cygne so that she could attend the local high school. Arlene was no relation to Ellison, but, according to his later statement, he came to look upon her as a member of the family.[267]

After Arlene Scott graduated from La Cygne High School in the spring of 1923, she secured a teaching job for the fall term in her home district of Centerville. She then moved to Pittsburg and enrolled for the summer term at the teacher's college there in order to obtain her temporary certificate.[268]

*Left*: J. Ellison Scott, accused wife murderer. *Right*: Eleanor "Ella" Scott, the murdered woman. *From the* St. Louis Post-Dispatch.

On the night of June 19, Ellison and Ella Scott attended a tent show in La Cygne and drove home in the family car, arriving about 11:00 p.m. They had been home just a few minutes when neighbors heard shots ring out, and a couple of minutes later, Scott appeared on the sidewalk outside the home exclaiming that his wife had been shot. By the time medical help arrived, though, Ella was beyond help and died minutes later from two gunshot wounds, one in each breast.[269]

At first, nearly everyone believed Ellison's story that he'd still been in the garage putting away the car when his wife was shot inside the house. The general supposition was that Ella Scott had interrupted a burglary in process. "You'll never make me believe Ellison Scott killed his wife, unless he admits it in court," one local man said, expressing the prevailing attitude. The Scotts' marriage had no outward signs of discord, and most people knew of no reason why Ellison might have wanted his wife dead.

But investigators were busy hunting up just such a motive.[270]

People were still skeptical even after Scott was arrested on June 22, three days after the shooting, because the county attorney and other officers would

# SCOTT ACCUSED OF WIFE'S MURDER

## Arrested Last Friday on Complaint of County Attorney

## RELEASED ON $15,000 BOND

Search for Revolver Continues Unabated and Confidence is Expressed that Missing Weapon Will be Found—Every Clue Being Traced.

Headline in a local newspaper tells the story of Ella Scott's murder. *From the* La Cygne (KS) Journal.

not reveal the nature of the incriminating evidence against the accused. Taken to Mound City, the county seat, and arraigned on a charge of first-degree murder, Scott pleaded not guilty and was released on $15,000 bond until his preliminary hearing.[271]

Meanwhile, Ella Scott's funeral was held in La Cygne on Friday, June 22, the same day her husband was arrested. Hundreds of people attended what was described as the largest funeral ever held in La Cygne, and Ella Scott's body was afterward interred at the local Oak Lawn Cemetery.[272]

At Ellison Scott's preliminary hearing before a justice of the peace on July 5, the accused was bound over for trial but released on $10,000 bond. His attorneys immediately filed a writ of habeas corpus in district court, seeking to have the charges dropped because of insufficient evidence. At the habeas corpus hearing on July 11, district judge Edward C. Gates refused to release the defendant but did order a new preliminary hearing with an admonition to the state that it needed to produce stronger evidence to justify holding Scott for trial.[273]

At Scott's new preliminary exam, held on July 27–28, "much damaging evidence against the accused was brought out" that was not presented at the first hearing, according to the *La Cygne Journal*, but even then there probably would not have been enough evidence to make a strong case against Scott "had it not been shown that he made a trip to Pittsburg a couple of weeks ago," met Arlene Scott, his deceased wife's niece, and registered with her at a hotel as man and wife under assumed names. Arlene Scott denied that she had ever been intimate with her uncle-in-law, but Sheriff L.J. Ellington, following her to the stand, testified that Arlene had admitted just such an affair to him less than a week earlier. Judge Gates ordered that Scott be held for trial under a $20,000 bond. Ellison Scott was unable to come up with the bail money, because the sensational testimony caused most of his supporters to desert him. He was, therefore, committed to the Linn County Jail at Mound City.[274]

When Scott's trial got underway at Mound City in mid-September, Judge Gates ruled that no one under the age of eighteen should be admitted to the courtroom, because of the spicy testimony regarding the intimacy between the defendant and Arlene Scott that was expected. County prosecutor W.W. Edeburn said he planned to show that Scott's motive for murdering his wife was twofold. He was financially embarrassed and hoped to collect on a $3,000 life insurance policy he'd taken out on Ella just a few months before her death. Also, he did not get along with his wife, contrary to the impression the couple gave in public, and he wanted to be free of her so that he could be with Arlene, with whom he had been carrying on an affair both before and after the murder.[275]

Edeburn introduced witnesses to establish that Scott was seen pacing back and forth inside his home within a minute after the fatal shots were fired and that he then appeared outside the home a minute or so later crying that his wife had been shot. Other witnesses were called to establish the likelihood of an affair between the defendant and Arlene Scott, including the proprietor of the Pittsburg hotel where the couple had registered and a former employee of the meat market that Scott operated in La Cygne. In addition, Edward Lee, who'd been a recent cell mate of Scott's at the county jail, testified that the defendant had confessed his intimate relations with Arlene to him.[276]

Arlene Scott, accused of having an affair with her aunt's husband. *From the* St. Louis Post-Dispatch.

The defense countered with witnesses who said that they'd seen a stranger very near the Scott home immediately after hearing the two fatal shots, that the relations between Scott and his wife were very congenial, and that Scott appeared sincerely grief-stricken in the aftermath of the murder. Scott's lawyers also introduced witnesses to impugn Edward Lee's reputation for truthfulness.[277]

Near the end of the trial, Ellison Scott took the stand in his own defense. He admitted going to the hotel in Pittsburg with his wife's niece, but he claimed he simply wanted to talk with her in private because he had been under such suspicion since his wife's death that Arlene was the only friend he had left. He said he wanted to get out of the public eye to protect Arlene's reputation, and he gave the same reason for registering as husband and wife. Asked why he didn't find some other private place to talk besides a hotel room, Scott said he had a bad headache and wanted to lie down. He admitted his actions were indiscreet, but he said he simply failed to consider the possible repercussions at the time. Asked why he had not picked his wife up or otherwise tried to attend to her when he found her dying on the floor, Scott gave the same excuse—that it simply hadn't occurred to him.[278]

On September 27, after deliberating for more than thirty hours, the jury in the Scott case failed to agree, and Judge Gates declared a mistrial. The jury stood eight to four in favor of acquittal. Gates set a new trial for the December term.[279]

After the hung jury, Linn County officials enlisted the aid of Kansas state attorney general Charles Griffith to prosecute Ellison Scott, and the case took a sensational turn in late November, when Griffith ordered Arlene arrested as an accessory to her aunt's murder. She was in the midst of her first term as a schoolteacher when she was taken into custody. At her preliminary hearing on December 1, Arlene was bound over for trial, jointly charged with Ellison Scott with the murder of Ella Scott. The trial was set for December 17, and Arlene was released on $5,000 bond until that time. Ellison Scott was also released on $10,000 bond. Many people speculated that the state had a very weak case against Arlene Scott and that the main reason for her arrest was to try to elicit new evidence against Ellison. Indeed, the state's main focus during the preliminary hearing was on proving a sexual intimacy between Ellison and his niece. For instance, one new witness, a kinsman of Arlene Scott, testified that she'd told him that Ellison Scott threatened to kill her if she revealed their affair.[280]

Defense attorneys filed a writ of habeas corpus with the Kansas Supreme Court seeking to have the charges against Arlene dropped, and her and Ellison Scott's trial was postponed until the motion could be heard. After the high court overruled Arlene's request in March 1924, her case was severed from Ellison Scott's. His new trial was set for April 22, while hers was postponed indefinitely pending the outcome of his.[281]

After a weeklong trial in late April, Ellison Scott was found guilty on May 1 of second-degree murder. Judge Gates overruled a defense motion for a new trial and sentenced the defendant to thirty years of hard labor at the state prison. Scott's lawyers then appealed to the state supreme court. On December 6, the high court overturned the verdict of the Linn County District Court and ordered a new trial. The supreme court held that Judge Gates had improperly disallowed certain defense evidence seeking to establish the presence of the stranger outside the Scott home on the night of the murder. The high court also said that, when a man was charged with murdering his wife, proof that he was intimate with another woman constituted legitimate evidence, but that mere circumstances suggesting that he might have had such an affair did not.[282]

Attorney General Griffith countered that there was insufficient evidence to entertain the theory of a burglar as Ella Scott's murderer, and he appealed to the supreme court for a rehearing on its ruling. The high court, however, affirmed its verdict in the spring of 1925, and Ellison Scott was released from the Linn County Jail on May 21 on bond after Judge Gates reduced the amount from $20,000 to $10,000.[283]

Scott was granted a change of venue for his third trial, which finally got underway in the Anderson County District Court at Garnett in March 1926. On the evening of March 16, the jury came back with a verdict of not guilty, but the news of Scott's final trial and his acquittal was not widely proclaimed. A case that had been hailed as the most sensational in Linn County history wound down with little publicity, and John Ellison Scott quietly walked away a free man.[284]

# NOTES

## Chapter One

1. *Lawrence (KS) Daily Journal*, June 3, 1870.
2. Ibid., May 20, 1870.
3. *Chanute (KS) Daily Tribune*, September 12, 1902, quoting *Topeka Mail and Breeze*.
4. *Lawrence Kansas Daily Tribune*, May 14, 1870, quoting *Fort Scott Monitor*; *Chanute Daily Tribune*, September 12, 1902; *Osage Mission (KS) Journal*, May 12, 1870.
5. *Lawrence Daily Journal*, June 3, 1870; *Chanute Daily Tribune*, September 12, 1902.
6. *Lawrence Daily Journal*, May 20, 21, June 3, 1870.
7. *Fort Scott Monitor*, May 13, 1870; *Chanute Daily Tribune*, September 12, 1902.
8. *Oswego Kansas Democrat*, May 26, 1870; *Chanute Daily Tribune*, September 12, 1902.
9. *Osage Mission Journal*, May 12, 1870; *Fort Scott Monitor*, May 13, 1870.
10. U.S. Census, 1870; Masterson, *Katy Railroad*, 56–57.
11. *Paola (KS) Miami Republican*, May 21, 1870, quoting *Fort Scott Monitor*; *Osage Mission Journal*, May 12, 1870.
12. *Fort Scott Daily Monitor*, May 13, 1870.
13. *Chanute Daily Tribune*, September. 12, 1902; *Chetopa (KS) Advance*, May 18, 1870.
14. *Osage Mission Journal*, May 12, 1870.

15. *Chanute Daily Tribune*, September 12, 1902; *Paola Miami Republican*, May 21, 1870, quoting *Fort Scott Monitor*.
16. *Chanute Daily Tribune*, September 12, 1902; *Paola Miami Republican*, May 21, 1870, quoting *Fort Scott Monitor*.
17. *Topeka Kansas State Record*, July 23, 1870; *Parsons (KS) Sun*, September 11, 2013.
18. U.S. Census, 1860, 1870; Kansas State Census, 1875; Find a Grave, https://www.findagrave.com/memorial/25743096/eliza-jane-talbott.
19. *Chetopa Advance*, May 18, 1870; *Osage Mission Journal*, May 12. 1870.
20. *Chanute Daily Tribune*, September 12, 1902.
21. *Osage Mission Journal*, May 26, 1870; *Parsons Sun*, September 11, 2013.

## Chapter Two

22. *Topeka Daily Commonwealth*, August 22, 1871.
23. *Emporia Weekly News*, August 25, 1871.
24. *Topeka State Record*, July 27, 1871.
25. *Topeka Daily Commonwealth*, August 15, 1871.
26. Ibid., August 15, 22, 1871.
27. Ibid., August, 15, 1871
28. *Topeka Kansas State Record*, August 14, 1871; *Topeka Daily Commonwealth*, August 15; *Emporia Weekly News*, August 15, 1871; Rosa, *Gunfighter*, 93. McCluskie's first name was sometimes given as Mike instead of William.
29. *Emporia Weekly News*, August 25, 1871; *Abilene Weekly Chronicle*, August 24, 1871; *Topeka Daily Commonwealth*, August 22, 1871.
30. *Abilene Weekly Chronicle*, August 24, 1871; *Topeka Daily Commonwealth*, August 22, 1871.
31. Muse, "History of Harvey County," 9.
32. *Topeka Daily Commonwealth*, August 22, 1871.
33. Ibid.
34. *Topeka Daily Commonwealth*, August 22, 23, 1871; *Abilene Weekly Chronicle*, August 24, 1871; *Emporia Weekly News*, August 25, 1871; Muse, "History of Harvey County," 9.
35. *Topeka Weekly Commonwealth*, August 30, 1871; Muse, "History of Harvey County," 9; Schmucker, "Texas Cowboy, Desperado, and Businessman."
36. *Newton Kansan*, August 7, 1873; *Topeka Daily Commonwealth*, August 9, 1873.

## Chapter Three

37. *Independence South Kansas Tribune*, April 2, 1873; *Girard (KS) Press*, April 2, 1873.

38. *Independence South Kansas Tribune*, March 11, 1873; *Thayer (KS) Head Light*, May 14, 1873; *Oswego (KS) Independent*, August 25, 1877, quoting its May 10, 1873 issue.

39. *Independence South Kansas Tribune*, April 2, 1873; *Girard Press*, April 2, 1873.

40. U.S. Census, 1870; *Council Grove Kansas Cosmos*, August 13, 1880, citing *Kansas City Times*.

41. *Chicago Tribune*, May 13, 1873; *Girard Press*, May 22, 1873; *Council Grove Kansas Cosmos*, August 13, 1880.

42. *Girard Press*, April 2, 1873; *Oswego Kansas Democrat*, April 25, 1873.

43. *Oswego Independent*, August 25, 1877, quoting its May 10, 1873 issue.

44. Ibid.

45. Ibid.

46. Ibid.

47. *Chicago Tribune*, May 13, 1873.

48. *Oswego Independent*, August 25, 1877, quoting its May 10, 1873 issue; *Council Grove Kansas Cosmos*, August 13, 1880. In an interesting sidelight, Brockman himself was convicted of murder twenty-five years later after his youngest daughter died from abuse and neglect.

49. *Girard Press*, May 22, 1873.

50. *Thayer Head Light*, May 14, 1873; *Fort Scott Daily Monitor*, May 20, 1873; *Lawrence Daily Journal*, May 11, 1873; *Lawrence Western Home Journal*, May 15, 1873.

51. *Girard Press*, May 15, 29, 1873; *Thayer Head Light*, May 7, 1873; *Fort Scott Daily Monitor*, May 20, 1873.

52. *Fort Scott Daily Monitor*, November 25, 1873; *Parsons Weekly Sun*, November 7, 1889; *Oswego Independent*, April 18, 1890, July 12, 1901.

53. *Wyandotte (KS) Gazette*, December 8, 1876; *Galena (KS) Miner*, August 20, 1880, citing the *Chicago Times*.

54. *Oswego Independent*, April 14, 1877; *Wichita Daily Eagle*, May 9, 1885.

## Chapter Four

55. *Topeka Daily Commonwealth*, October 15, 1872.

56. *Wichita Beacon*, February 15, 1899.

57. U.S. Census, 1870 census; Rosa and, Koop, *Rowdy Joe Lowe*, 20–35.
58. Rosa and Koop, *Rowdy Joe Lowe*, 43; *Lawrence Daily Record*, September 27, 1871, quoting *Topeka Record*; *Topeka Daily Commonwealth*, June 6, 1872.
59. *Wichita Eagle*, November 27, 1873; U.S. Census, 1860, 1870.
60. *Wichita Eagle*, June 5, 1873; Rosa and Koop, *Rowdy Joe Lowe*, 78.
61. Rosa and Koop, *Rowdy Joe Lowe*, 79; *Wichita Beacon*, February 15, 1899.
62. Rosa and Koop, *Rowdy Joe Lowe*, 79–80, 86; *Winfield (KS) Courier*, October 30, 1873.
63. *Wichita Eagle*, October 30, 1873; Rosa and Koop, *Rowdy Joe Lowe*, 81–82.
64. Rosa and Koop, *Rowdy Joe Lowe*, 82; *Wichita Eagle*, October 30, 1873.
65. *Wichita Eagle*, October 30, November 13, 1873; *Iola (KS) Register*, November 15, 1873.
66. *Wichita Eagle*, December 18, 1873.
67. Ibid., January 8, 1874; Records of the Kansas State Penitentiary, https:// www.kshs.org/archives/214393.
68. *Wichita Eagle*, January, 15, 1874; *Wichita Beacon*, February 16, 1899; Rosa and Koop, *Rowdy Joe Lowe*, 97, 107–111.

## Chapter Five

69. *Valley Falls (KS) Register*, January 12, 1883; *Winfield Courier*, February 1, 1883.
70. *Valley Falls Register*, January 12, 1883.
71. *Oskaloosa (KS) Weekly Sickle*, January 13, 1883; *Valley Falls New Era*, January 20, 1883.
72. *Oskaloosa Independent*, January 20, 1883; *Winfield Courier*, January 18, 1883.
73. *Winfield Courier*, January 25, 1883.
74. Ibid., January 25, February 1, 1883.
75. Ibid., January 25, 1883.
76. Ibid.
77. Ibid., January 25, 1883; *Wichita Eagle*, January 25, 1883.
78. *Winfield Courier*, January 25, 1883.
79. Ibid.
80. Ibid.
81. Ibid.
82. Ibid.
83. Ibid.
84. Ibid.

85. Ibid.
86. Ibid.
87. Ibid.
88. *Winfield Courier*, February 1, 1883.
89. *Wichita Daily Times*, January 27, 1883; *Winfield Courier*, February 1, 1883.
90. *Wichita Daily Times*, January 27, 1883.
91. Ibid.
92. *Winfield Courier*, February 1, 1883.
93. Ibid.
94. Ibid.
95. Ibid.
96. *Winfield Courier*, February 1, 8, 22, 1883.
97. Ibid., February 1, 1883.
98. Ibid.
99. Ibid.
100. *Winfield Courier*, February 8, 1883.
101. Ibid.
102. *Wichita Eagle*, February 8, 1883.
103. *Wichita Daily Times*, February 2, 1883.
104. *Winfield Courier*, February 22, 1883.
105. Ibid.

## Chapter Six

106. *Wichita Daily Eagle*, August 14, 1884.
107. Reinhardt, *Workin' on the Railroad*, 100. The LL&G Railroad had been acquired by the Kansas City, Lawrence and Southern by this time, but it was still often called the LL&G.
108. Ibid.
109. Ibid., 100–101.
110. Metz, *Encyclopedia of Lawmen*, 203.
111. Halsell, *Cowboys and Cattleland*.
112. Ibid.; U.S. Census, 1860; *Caldwell (KS) Advance*, August 14, 1884.
113. *Wellington (KS) Wellingtonian*, August 14, 1884.
114. *Caldwell Advance*, August 14, 1884.
115. Ibid., August 14, 1884; *Wellington (KS) Wellingtonian*, August 14, 1884; Halsell, *Cowboys and Cattleland*.
116. *Wichita Daily Eagle*, August 14, 1884; Halsell, *Cowboys and Cattleland*.

117. *Topeka State Journal*, August 19, 1884.

118. Halsell, *Cowboys and Cattleland*; *Darlington (OK) Cheyenne Transporter*, August 30, 1884.

119. *Caldwell Advance*, September 4, 1884.

120. Dary, *Stories of Old-Time Oklahoma*, 132–133; *Vinita (OK) Daily Chieftain*, August 16, 1909; Halsell, *Cowboys and Cattleland*; "Oscar D. Halsell," Find a Grave, https://www.findagrave.com/memorial/44008358/oscar-d.-halsell.

121. Metz, *Encyclopedia of Lawmen*, 203; "Hamilton Polk Rayner," Find a Grave, https://www.findagrave.com/memorial/120427794/hamilton-polk-rayner.

122. "Kansas Post Offices, 1828–1961"; "Cowtowns," *Kansapedia*.

## Chapter Seven

123. *Emporia Daily News*, July 23, 1885; *Emporia Republican*, July 30, 1885.

124. *Emporia Republican*, December 18, 1884; *Emporia Democrat*, May 7, 1884; *Emporia Daily News*, October 29, 1885.

125. *New Orleans Times-Picayune*, August 23, 1885.

126. *Emporia Daily News*, July 20, 1885; *New-Orleans Times-Picayne*, August 23, 1885.

127. *Emporia News*, August 22, 1885.

128. Ibid., August 25, 1885.

129. *Emporia Daily News*, August 24, 25, 1885; *New Orleans Weekly Times-Democrat*, August 29, 1885.

130. *Emporia Daily News*, August 24–29, 1885.

131. Ibid., August 31, September 1, September 7, 1885.

132. Ibid., October 20–24, 1885.

133. Ibid., October 26–28, 1885.

134. Ibid., October 29–30, 1885.

135. Ibid., November 6–7, 10, 1885; *Emporia Democrat*, November 11, 1885.

136. *Emporia Daily News*, November 18, 1885.

137. Ibid., November 12, 1885; *Emporia Weekly News*, August 16, 1888, quoting *Chicago Times*.

138. *Chicago Tribune*, November 15, 28, 1897.

139. Ibid., December 26, 1897, April 29, 1898; *Chicago Inter Ocean*, February 2, 1898.

140. *Chicago Tribune*, April 18, 19, 1914; *Chicago Inter Ocean*, April 19, 1914;

*Lyon County News and Emporia Times*, April 23, 1914.

141. "Minnie Estelle Wallace Keating," Find a Grave, https://www.findagrave.com/memorial/169506226/minnie-estelle-keating.


## Chapter Eight

142. *Coffeyville (KS) Weekly Journal*, October 7, 1892.
143. U.S. Census, 1860, 1870; "Adeline Lee Dalton," Genealogy-Geni.
144. *Coffeyville Weekly Journal*, July 19, 1889, May 15, 1891; *Fort Worth Gazette*, May 16, 1891.
145. *Coffeyville Weekly Journal*, July 29, October 7, 1892.
146. Ibid., September 30, October 7, 1892.
147. Ibid., October 7, 1892.
148. Ibid.
149. Ibid.
150. Ibid.
151. Ibid.
152. Ibid.
153. Ibid.
154. Ibid.
155. Ibid.
156. Ibid.
157. Ibid.
158. Ibid.
159. Ibid
160. Presland, "Emmett Dalton Timeline."


## Chapter Nine

161. The original German spelling of Staffleback was "Staffelbach," but I've adopted the Anglicized spelling, which was commonly used in newspaper reports about the family. See the *St. Louis Post-Dispatch*, September 14, 1897, for an example of a paper that called the Stafflebacks "worse than the Benders."
162. *Galena Evening Times*, July 19, 1897.
163. Ibid., July 20, 22, 1897.
164. *Pittsburg (KS) Daily Headlight*, July 29, 1987, quoting *Joplin (MO) News*.

165. U.S. Census, 1860, 1870, 1880; *Joplin Daily Herald*, July 28, 1878; *Mount Vernon Lawrence Chieftain*, September 8, 1887, December 12, 1889, September 6, 1894, March 21, 1895; *Galena Evening Times*, July 30, 1897; Missouri State Penitentiary database.

166. *Joplin Daily Herald*, July 29, 1897.

167. *Columbus (KS) Daily Advocate*, July 13, 1897; *Joplin Daily Herald*, July 29, 1897; *Galena Evening Times*, July 28 1897.

168. *Joplin Daily Herald*, July 29, 1897; *Galena Evening Times*, July 28, 1897.

169. *Joplin Daily Herald*, July 29, 1897; *Galena Evening Times*, July 28, 1897.

170. *Joplin Daily Herald*, July 29, 1897; *Galena Evening Times*, July 28, 1897.

171. *Joplin Daily Herald*, July 29, 1897; *Galena Evening Times*, July 28, 1897.

172. *Joplin Daily Herald*, July 29, 1897; *Galena Evening Times*, July 28, 1897.

173. *Joplin Daily Herald*, July 29, 1897; *Galena Evening Times*, July 28, 1897; *Columbus Daily Advocate*, June 21, 1897.

174. *Galena Evening Times*, July 29, 1897; *Joplin Daily Herald*, July 29, 1897.

175. *Galena Evening Times*, September 13, 14, 15, 1897; *Columbus Courier*, September 16, 1897; *Galena Times*, September 17, 1897.

176. *Galena Evening Times*, September 15, 1897; *Columbus Courier*, September 16, 1897.

177. *Galena Evening Times*, September 15, 1897.

178. *Columbus Courier*, September 16, 1897.

179. *Galena Weekly Republican*, September 18, 1897; *Galena Evening Times*, September 28, 1897.

180. *St. Louis Republic*, September 19, 1897.

181. *Galena Evening Times*, September 21, 1897.

182. *Columbus Courier*, September 23, 1897; *Columbus Daily Advocate*, September 29, 1987.

183. *Galena Evening Times*, October 1, 1897.

184. Ibid., October 2, 1897; *Columbus Weekly Advocate*, October 7, 1897.

185. *Galena Times*, April 1, 22, 1898.

186. *Columbus Daily Advocate*, November 18, 1899; *Galena Evening Times*, March 10, 1909; *Columbus Weekly Advocate*, August 14, 1902; *Galena Weekly Republican*, October 27, 1898.

## Chapter Ten

187. U.S. Census, 1900; *El Dorado (KS) Daily Republican*, June 22, 1900.

188. *El Dorado Daily Republican*, July 18, 1900.

189. Ibid., July 18, 20, 1900

190. Ibid., June 22, 1900.

191. Ibid.

192. Ibid.

193. *El Dorado Walnut Valley Times*, June 22, 1900.

194. *El Dorado Daily Republican*, June 29, 1900; *El Dorado Walnut Valley Times*, July 10, 1900.

195. *El Dorado Butler County Democrat*, June 29, 1900.

196. *El Dorado Daily Republican*, June 22, 1900.

197. Ibid., July 22, 1900; *El Dorado Walnut Valley Times*, June 24, July 10, 1902.

198. *El Dorado Daily Republican*, July 6, 1900.

199. *El Dorado Walnut Valley Times*, July 10, 11, 1900.

200. *El Dorado Daily Republican*, July 17–20, 1900.

201. Ibid., July 21, 23, 24, 1900; *El Dorado Republican*, August 17, 1900.

202. *El Dorado Republican*, November 23, 1900; *El Dorado Daily Republican*, November 30, December 1, 4, 1900.

203. *El Dorado Walnut Valley Times*, December 7, 1900; *El Dorado Republican*, December 10, 1900.

204. *El Dorado Republican*, December 14, 1900.

205. Ibid., June 21, 1901.

206. Ibid., June 14, 21, 28, 1901; *Topeka Daily Capital*, June 28, 1901; *El Dorado Walnut Valley Times*, January 3, 1902.

207. *El Dorado Walnut Valley Times*, July 1, 6, 9, 1901.

208. *El Dorado Butler County Democrat*, September 13, 1901; *Reports of Cases Argued and Determined in the Supreme Court of the State of Kansas*, 669–681.

209. *El Dorado Walnut Valley Times*, June 24, 28, July 8, 13, 1902.

210. Ibid., September 26, 1902; *El Dorado Republican*, October 7, 1902, May 15, June 12, 1903; *El Dorado Daily Republican*, June 11, 1903.

211. *El Dorado Walnut Valley Times*, September 29, 1910; *El Dorado Republican*, September 30, 1910.

212. *El Dorado Republican*, September 30, 1903, August 11, 1911; *El Dorado Walnut Valley Times*, February 28, 1913.

213. *El Dorado Walnut Valley Times*, February 28, 1913; *El Dorado Republican*, October 5, 1923.

## Chapter Eleven

214. *Wichita Daily Eagle,* June 24, 1904.
215. Ibid.
216. *Wichita Daily Eagle,* July 3, 16, 23, 1904; U.S. Census, 1900.
217. *Wichita Daily Eagle,* June 24, 1904.
218. Ibid.; *Wichita Beacon,* June 23, 1904.
219. *Wichita Daily Eagle,* June 24, 1904.
220. Ibid.
221. Ibid.
222. Ibid.
223. Ibid.
224. Ibid.
225. Ibid.
226. Ibid.
227. Ibid.
228. Ibid.
229. *Wichita Daily Eagle,* June 25, 1904.
230. Ibid., June 26, 1904.
231. Ibid., July 3, 16, 1904.
232. *Wichita Beacon,* July 22, 1904; *Wichita Daily Eagle,* July 23, 1904.
233. *Wichita Beacon,* July 22, 1904; *Wichita Daily Eagle,* July 23, 1904.

## Chapter Twelve

234. *Iola Register,* September 28, 1907.
235. Ibid., October 16, 1907.
236. *Fort Scott Weekly Monitor,* July 14, 1897; *Iola Register,* October 16, 1907.
237. *Iola Register,* September 30, 1907.
238. Ibid., September 28, October 7, 1907.
239. Ibid.
240. *Iola Register,* September 28, 30, 1907; *Topeka State Journal,* September 30, 1907.
241. *Iola Register,* September 28, 30, 1907.
242. Ibid., September 28, 1907; *Topeka State Journal,* September 30, 1907.
243. *Topeka State Journal,* September 30, 1907; *Independence (KS) Evening Star,* September 30, 1907.
244. *Iola Register,* September 28, 1907.

245. Ibid., September 30, 1907.

246. Ibid.

247. *Iola Register*, September 30, 1907; *Topeka State Journal*, September 30, 1907.

248. *Iola Register*, October 1, 1907; *Chanute Daily Tribune*, October 2, 1907.

249. *Iola Register*, October 8, 1907.

250. Ibid.

251. Ibid.

252. *Iola Register*, October 8, 1907; *St. Louis Post-Dispatch*, October 8, 1907.

253. *Iola Register*, October 9, 1907.

254. *St. Louis Post-Dispatch*, October 9, 1907; *Iola Register*, October 9, 1907.

255. *Iola Register*, October, 10, 1907.

256. Ibid., October 11, 1907.

257. Ibid.

258. Ibid.

259. *Iola Register*, October 15–16, 1907.

260. Ibid., October 24–25, 29, November 1, 1907.

261. Ibid., January 14, May 22, 1908.

262. Ibid., May 18–29, 1908.

263. Ibid., May 18–31, 1908.

264. Ibid., May 31, 1908.

265. Ibid., July 14, September 25, 1908.

## *Chapter Thirteen*

266. *La Cygne (KS) Journal*, August 3, 1923.

267. *La Cygne Journal*, August 3, December 7, 1923.

268. Ibid., August 3, 1923.

269. Ibid., December 7, 1923; *Iola Register*, September 19, 1923.

270. *La Cygne Journal*, June 29, 1923.

271. Ibid.

272. Ibid.

273. *La Cygne Journal*, July 20, 1923.

274. Ibid., August 3, 1923.

275. *Iola Register*, September 17, 18, 1923.

276. Ibid., September 19, 20, 1923.

277. Ibid., September 21, 22, 1923.

278. Ibid., September 24, 1923.

279. Ibid., September 27, 1923.

280. *Fort Scott Tribune and Monitor*, December 6 1923; *La Cygne Journal*, December 7, 1923.

281. *La Cygne Journal*, February 1, March 14, 21, April 22, 1924.

282. Ibid., May 9, 16, 1924; *Hutchinson (KS) News*, December 6, 1924.

283. *Hutchinson News*, March 4, May 21, 1925.

284. Ibid., August 1, 1925; *Joplin (MO) Globe*, March 17, 1926.

# BIBLIOGRAPHY

"Adeline Lee Dalton." Genealogy-Geni. https://www.geni.com/people/Adeline-Dalton/6000000003590106217.

"Cowtowns." *Kansapedia.* Kansas Historical Society. https://www.kshs.org/kansapedia/cowtowns/15598.

Dary, David. *Stories of Old-Time Oklahoma.* Norman: University of Oklahoma Press, 2011.

Find a Grave, https://www.findagrave.com.

Halsell, H.H. *Cowboys and Cattleland.* Nashville, TN: Parthenon Press, 1937. Reprint, Bordino Books, 2017.

"Kansas Post Offices, 1828–1961," Kansas Historical Society. https://www.kshs.org/index.php?url=geog/geog_postoffices/search/page:2/county:SU.

Kansas State Census. www.FamilySearch.org.

Masterson, V.V. *The Katy Railroad and the Last Frontier.* 1952. Reprint, Columbia: University of Missouri Press, 1988.

Metz, Leon Claire. *The Encyclopedia of Lawmen, Outlaws, and Gunfighters.* New York: Facts on File, 2003.

Missouri State Penitentiary. Missouri State Archives. https://s1.sos.mo.gov/records/archives/archivesdb/msp.

Muse, R.W.P. "History of Harvey County" in *Historical Atlas of Harvey County, Kansas.* Philadelphia: John P. Edwards, 1882.

Presland, Kith M. "Emmett Dalton Timeline." http://www.kayempea.net/adds/timeline.htm.

Records of the Kansas State Penitentiary, Kansas State Historical Society. https://www.kshs.org/archives.

Reinhardt, Richard, ed. *Workin' on the Railroad: Reminiscences from the Age of Steam*. Norman: University of Oklahoma Press, 1970.

*Reports of Cases Argued and Determined in the Supreme Court of the State of Kansas.* Thomas Emmet Dewey, reporter. Topeka, KS: W.Y. Morgan, 1902.

Rosa, Joseph G. *The Gunfighter: Man or Myth?* Norman: University of Oklahoma Press, 1969.

Rosa, Joseph G., and Waldo E. Koop. *Rowdy Joe Lowe: Gambler with a Gun.* Norman: University of Oklahoma Press, 1989.

Schmucker, Kristine. "Texas Cowboy, Desperado, and Businessman: Hugh Anderson." Harvey County Historical Museum. http://hchm.org/texas-cowboy-desperado-businessman-hugh-anderson.

U.S. Census records. www.FamilySearch.org.

# ABOUT THE AUTHOR

 arry Wood is a retired public schoolteacher and a freelance writer specializing in the history of the Ozarks and surrounding areas. He is the author of two historical novels and sixteen nonfiction books on regional history, including seven published by The History Press. Wood's books, stories, and articles have won numerous awards from organizations like the Ozark Writers' League, the Ozark Creative Writers, and the Missouri Writers' Guild. In 2016, he was named an honorary lifetime member of the latter organization. Wood maintains a blog on regional history at www.ozarks-history.blogspot.com.

*Visit us at*
www.historypress.com
..............................................................

Printed in the USA
CPSIA information can be obtained
at www.ICGtesting.com
LVHW050231040124
767839LV00043B/1225